CHILTON'S Repair and Tune-Up Guide

Chevrolet LUV

1972-75

ILLUSTRATED

Prepared by the

Automotive Editorial Department

Chilton Book Company

Chilton Way
Radnor, Pa. 19089
215—687-8200

president and chief executive officer **WILLIAM A. BARBOUR;** executive vice president **RICHARD H. GROVES;** vice president and general manager **WILLIAM D. BYRNE;** associate editorial director **GLEN B. RUH;** managing editor **JOHN H. WEISE, S.A.E.;** assistant managing editor **PETER J. MEYER, S.A.E.;** senior editor **KERRY A. FREEMAN;** editor **ROBERT J. BROWN**

CHILTON BOOK COMPANY　　　　　RADNOR, PENNSYLVANIA

Library of Congress Cataloging in Publication Data

Chilton Book Company. Automotive Editorial Dept.
  Chilton's repair and tune-up guide, Chevrolet LUV
1972–75.

  1. Chevrolet LUV truck. I. Title. II. Title: Re-
pair and tune-up guide, Chevrolet LUV 1972–75.
TL230.5.C45C47   1975   629.28'7'3   74-26617
ISBN 0-8019-6200-5
ISBN 0-8019-6201-3 pbk.

ACKNOWLEDGMENTS

Chilton Book Company expresses appreciation to the following
for their cooperation and technical assistance:

Chevrolet Motor Division
General Motors Corporation
Detroit, Michigan

Hickey Enterprises, Inc.
1645 Callens Road
Ventura, California 93003

Pioneer Chevrolet
Wayne, Pennsylvania 19087

Information in this book has been selected from Chevrolet LUV
shop manuals, Chevrolet LUV owner's manuals and Chevrolet
Motor Division promotional materials.

Although the information in this guide is based on industry
sources and is as complete as possible at the time of publication,
the possibility exists that the manufacturer made later changes
which could not be included here. While striving for total accu-
racy, Chilton Book Company cannot assume responsibility for
any errors, changes, or omissions that may occur in the compila-
tion of this data.

Contents

Chapter 1   General Information and Maintenance 1

How to Use This Book, 1
History, 1
Model Identification, 2
Serial Number Identification, 2
Routine Maintenance, 2

Capacities Chart, 6
Lubrication, 8
Bearing Failure Chart, 12
Pushing, Towing, and Jump Starting, 17
Jacking and Hoisting, 18

Chapter 2   Tune-Up and Troubleshooting 19

Tune-Up Procedures, 19
Tune-Up Specifications Chart, 20

Tune-Up and Troubleshooting, 29

Chapter 3   Engine and Engine Rebuilding 46

Engine Electrical, 46
Firing Order Illustration, 47
Alternator and Regulator Specifications
    Chart, 48
Battery and Starter Specifications Chart,
    49
Engine Mechanical, 50
General Engine Specifications Chart, 51
Valve Specifications Chart, 51
Crankshaft and Connecting Rod Specifi-
    cations Chart, 51

Ring   Side   Clearance   Specifications
    Chart, 51
Torque Specifications Chart, 51
Ring Gap Specifications Chart, 52
Piston Clearance Specifications Chart, 52
Engine Lubrication, 59
Engine Cooling, 60
Engine Rebuilding, 62

Chapter 4   Emission Controls and Fuel System 84

Emission Controls, 84
Fuel System, 92

Carburetor Specifications Chart, 97

Chapter 5   Chassis Electrical 99

Heater, 99
Radio, 101
Windshield Wipers, 101

Instrument Cluster, 101
Lighting, 102
Wiring Diagrams, 102

Chapter 6   Clutch and Transmission 108

Manual Transmission, 108

Clutch, 109

Chapter 7   Drive Train 114

Driveline, 114
Rear Axle, 114
Differential, 116

General Drive Axle Diagnostic Guide,
    121
Axle Noise Diagnosis Chart, 122

Chapter 8   Suspension and Steering 123

Front Suspension, 123
Wheel Alignment Specifications Chart,
    129

Rear Suspension, 130
Steering, 132

iii

Chapter 9   Brakes 133

Brake System, 133   Rear Drum Brakes, 139
Hydraulic System, 134   Parking Brake, 141
Front Drum Brakes, 137   Brake Specifications Chart, 142

Chapter 10   Body 143

Doors, 143   Fuel Tank, 145
Hood, 144

Appendix 146

1 · General Information and Maintenance

How to Use This Book

This book is written to help the Chevy LUV owner in performing maintenance, tune-ups and repairs on his vehicle. It will be helpful to both the amateur and experienced mechanic. Information on simple operations and more complex ones is given, allowing the user to try procedures which he or she feels confident in doing and graduating to the more difficult tasks as more experience is gained.

In addition to this book, a willingness to do your own work, and the time to do it right, there are a few other items you will have to be aware that you will need. A basic but complete set of metric hand tools is a must. For many repair operations the factory recommends special tools be used. A conventional tool can be substituted for the special tool in a lot of cases. For those operations requiring a special tool for which no substitution can be made, this fact is called to your attention in the text. Remember that whenever the left-side of the vehicle is referred to, it is the driver's side of the car and vice versa. Also, most screws and bolts are removed by turning them counterclockwise and tightened by turning them clockwise. Left-handed threads (the opposite of above) will be brought to your attention in the text.

Before you start any project, read the entire section in the book that deals with the particular job you wish to perform. Many times a description of the system and its operation is given. This will enable you to understand the function of the system you will be working on and what must be done to fix it. Reading the procedures beforehand will help you avoid problems and to learn about your Chevy LUV while you are working on it.

The more you work on your LUV and the more experienced you become, you will gain more confidence and appreciate this Repair and Tune-Up Guide.

History

The Chevy LUV was introduced in 1972 (model year). Designed to compete with the Japanese imports, the LUV itself is made by a Japanese automobile manufacturer, Izuzu Motors.

Model Identification

Chevy LUV pickup

There is only one model of the Chevy LUV: ½ ton conventional design powered by a water-cooled 110.8 cu in. (1817 cc) 4 cylinder inline single overhead camshaft gasoline engine with a 102.4 in. wheelbase and a 6 ft cargo bed. A Mikado version of the LUV is mainly an optional trim package.

Serial Number Identification

VEHICLE

The chassis number plate is attached to the left-side rear door pillar within the cab. It has the date of production and chassis number stamped on its face.

ENGINE

The engine number is stamped on the right upper center part of the cylinder block, adjacent to the distributor.

Location of the chassis number plate on the left-side rear door pillar

Routine Maintenance

AIR CLEANER

The air filter is the wet-element type. It is recommended that the element be replaced every 24,000 miles or sooner if the vehicle is operated in dusty areas. To replace the air cleaner element, simply unscrew the wing nut on the top of the air cleaner, disconnect the rubber hoses from the clip on the cover, and disconnect the rubber hose from the vacuum motor. Then, remove the bracket bolts at the air cleaner cover and lift the cover off. Lift the old element out and install the new element. Reassemble the air cleaner cover to the air cleaner assembly in the reverse order of removal.

Location of the engine identification number on the center of the right-side of the cylinder block

PCV VALVE

The positive crankcase ventilation (PCV) valve is to be replaced every 12,000 miles. Inspect the PCV system hoses and connections for proper con-

Removing the air cleaner

nections as well as condition at the time of replacement of the PCV valve. Blow out the hose with compressed air and replace any damaged or deteriorated hose.

FUEL EVAPORATIVE EMISSIONS SYSTEM

Check the evaporation control system every 12,000 miles. Check the fuel and vapor lines and hoses for proper connections and correct routing as well as condition. Replace damaged or deteriorated parts as necessary. Remove and check the operation of the check valve in the following manner:

1. When air is applied from the fuel tank side: The check valve is normal if air passes into the check side (crankcase side) but not leaking into the relief side (air cleaner side).

2. When air is applied from the check valve side: The valve is normal if the passage of air is restricted.

3. When air is applied from the relief side (air cleaner side): The valve is normal if air passes into the fuel tank side but not leaking into the check side (crankcase side).

BELTS

Check the belts driving the fan, air pump, air conditioning compressor and generator for cracks, fraying, wear and tension every 6,000 miles. It is recommended that the belts be replaced every

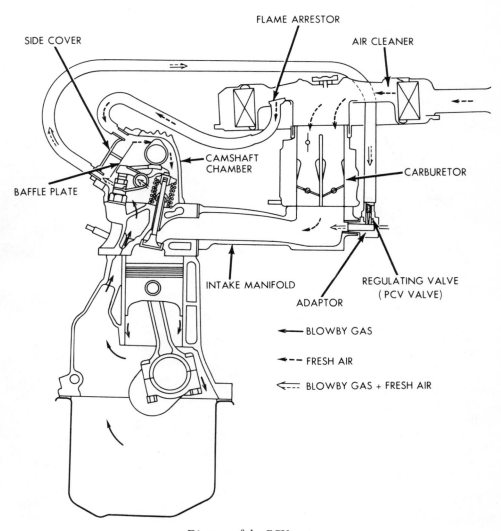

Diagram of the PCV system

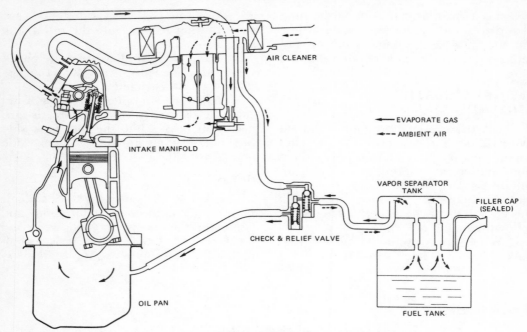

Diagram of the fuel evaporative emission control system

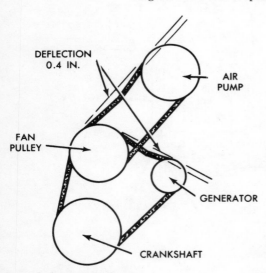

Drive belt tension adjustment

Air pump drive belt adjusting bolt

24 months or 24,000 miles, whichever comes first. Belt deflection midway between the two farthest pulleys should be no more than $7/16$ in. The drive belts are adjusted by loosening the component which the belt is driving and moving the component away from the engine.

AIR CONDITIONING

Check all of the air conditioning hoses for tight connections. Look for oil-type

Alternator drive belt adjusting bolt

stains at the connecting points which would indicate escaping refrigerant. Make sure that all metal tubing lines are free of kinks. Flexible lines should never be bent to a radius of less than four times the diameter of the hose. Also, all hoses should be kept at least 2½ in. from the exhaust manifold. Any hoses found to be deteriorated should be replaced at once.

Brake fluid level markings on the master cylinder reservoirs. The clutch reservoir has the same markings and is located at the right in the illustration

FLUID CHECKS

Engine Oil

The best time to check the engine oil is before operating the engine or after it has been sitting for at least 10 minutes in order to gain an accurate reading. This will allow the oil to drain back in the crankcase. To check the engine oil level, make sure that the vehicle is resting on a level surface, remove the oil dipstick, wipe it clean and reinsert the stick firmly for an accurate reading. The oil dip-stick has two holes to indicate high and low oil level. If the oil is at or below the "low level" hole in the dipstick, oil should be added as necessary. The oil level should be maintained in the safety margin, neither going above the "high level" hole or below the "low level" hole.

Transmission

Check the level of the lubricant in the transmission every 6,000 miles. The lubricant level should be maintained to the bottom of the filler hole. Hold in on the filler plug when unscrewing it. When you are sure that all of the threads of the plug are free of the transmission case, move the plug away from the case slightly. If lubricant begins to flow out of the transmission, then you know it is full. If not, add SAE 30 engine oil as necessary. It is recommended the transmission lubricant be changed every 24,000 miles.

Brake and Clutch Master Cylinder

Check the levels of brake fluid in the brake and clutch master cylinder reservoirs every 3,000 miles. The fluid level should be maintained to a level not below the bottom line on the reservoirs and not above the top line. Any sudden decrease in the level in either of the three reservoirs (two for the brakes and one for the clutch) indicates a probable leak in that particular system and the possibility of a leak should be checked out.

Coolant

Check the coolant level every time you change the oil. Check for loose connections and signs of deterioration of the coolant hoses. Maintain a level of coolant to within 3 in. below the level of the filler neck when the engine is cold. Add a mixture of 50% water and 50% ethylene glycol antifreeze as necessary. Never remove the radiator cap when the vehicle is hot or overheated. Wait until it has cooled. Place a thick cloth over the radiator cap to shield yourself from the heat and turn the radiator cap *slightly* until the sound of escaping pressure can be heard. *Do not turn any farther.* Allow the pressure to release gradually. When no more pressure can be heard escaping, then remove the cap with the heavy cloth *cautiously.* Never add cold water to an overheated engine while the engine is not running. Run the engine until it reaches normal operating temperature after filling the radiator to make sure that the thermostat has opened and all air is bled from the system.

Rear Axle

Check the rear axle lubricant every 6,000 miles.

Replace the rear axle lubricant after the first 600 miles and every 24,000 miles afterward. If the vehicle is operated in exceptionally heavy work or

Capacities

Year	Engine No. Cyl Displacement cu in. (cc)	Transmission Pts to Refill After Draining	Drive Axle (pts)	Gas Tank (gals)	Cooling System (qts) With Heater	Without Heater
1972–75	4-110.8 (1817 cc)	2.6	2.7	10①	6.4	5.3

① 13.2 gals in 1974–75

at continuous high-speeds, the lubricant should be changed every 12,000 miles.

To check the rear axle lubricant level, remove the filler plug in the axle housing. The lubricant should be up to the bottom of the filler hole with the vehicle resting on a level surface. Add SAE 90 hypoid gear oil as necessary to bring the lubricant up to the proper level.

Steering Gear

Check the level of lubricant in the steering gear every 12,000 miles. If the level is low, check for leakage. An oily film is not considered a leak; solid grease must be present. Change the lubricant every 36,000 miles. Use steering gear lubricant. The capacity of the steering gear is 10 fluid ounces.

Battery

Check the level of the electrolyte in the battery once a month. The level should be maintained up to the square section of the filler hole necks. Use only colorless, odorless drinking water or distilled water to bring the electrolyte up to the proper level.

In freezing weather, it is recommended that the vehicle be driven after adding water to the battery in order to properly mix the electrolyte and prevent freezing.

TIRES AND WHEELS

Every 3,000 miles check the tires for excessive wear, nails, glass, cuts or other damage. Make sure that the wheels are not bent or cracked and the wheel nuts are tight. Uneven or abnormal tire wear may indicate the need for front end alignment. Check the tire inflation pressure at least once a month or more often if you notice that the tires seem low. Truck type tires should be replaced when the tread depth becomes $1/16$ in. or less.

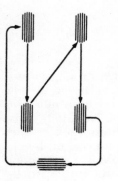 

5 WHEELS **4 WHEELS**

Tire rotation diagram

Tire Rotation

Tires should be rotated every 6,000 miles. If no spare is used, follow the "rotating four tires" diagram. If you have a spare and are including it in your tire rotating sequence, follow the "rotating five tires" diagram.

If uneven tire wear occurs before 6,000 miles, rotate the tires sooner. If the tires show abnormal wear patterns, have the axle alignment checked. Inflation pressures should be adjusted whenever tires are rotated. Tires should also be balanced or rebalanced when they are rotated.

Tire Life and Safety

Common sense and good driving habits will afford maximum tire life. Fast starts and stops, and hard cornering are hard on tires and will shorten their useful life span. If you start at normal speeds, allow yourself sufficient time to stop, and take corners at a reasonable speed, the life of your tires will increase greatly. Also make sure that you don't overload your vehicle or run with incorrect pressure in the tires. Both of these practices increase tread wear.

Inspect your tires frequently. Be especially careful to watch for bubbles in the tread or side wall, deep cuts, or underinflation. Remove any tires with bubbles. If the cuts are so deep they penetrate to the cords, discard the tire. Also look for uneven tread wear patterns that indicate that the front end is out of alignment or that the tires are out of balance.

Wider Treads and Radial Ply Tires

The main thing to remember when you have decided to install a different type tire on your vehicle is that you have to install at least four. Your spare tire should be of the same size and tread design as the rest.

Radial tires must not be mixed with belted or conventional tires because of the unusual handling characteristics that will result. Radial tires are not designed for vehicles that carry a substantial load, once again, because of the unusual handling characteristics that will result. Make sure that the tires you select will provide adequate clearance between the fender wells, the fenders themselves, and all suspension and steering components. Also, oversize flotation type tires require wider rims than stock.

Mud and snow tires should be operated at full inflation pressures and not at sustained speeds over 75 mph for one hour or more.

FUEL FILTER

A fuel filter is located in the fuel line leading from the fuel tank to the fuel pump. It is of the cartridge type with a paper filter element. If the fuel line is suspected of being clogged, check the fuel filter. Otherwise, the filter never has to be serviced.

BATTERY CARE

Maintain the battery electrolyte level, as outlined in the fluid level section, above.

If the terminals become corroded, clean them with a solution of baking soda mixed with water. Wash off the top of the battery with this solution and then rinse it off using clean, clear water.

CAUTION: *Be sure the filler caps are on tight or the electrolyte in the battery may become contaminated.*

Use petroleum jelly or silicone lubricant to protect the battery terminals. Check to be sure that the cables are fastened securely at both ends. Also, be sure that the battery hold-down bracket nuts are secure and free of corrosion.

When installing a new battery, be sure that its amp/hour capacity is at least as high as that of the battery which was re-

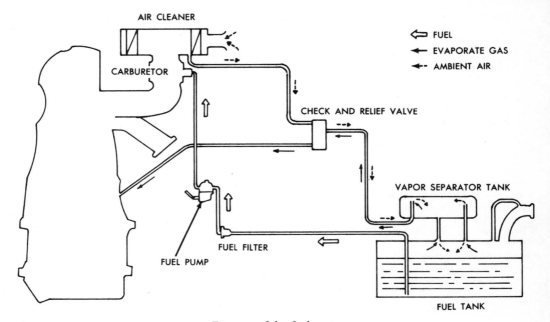

Diagram of the fuel system

moved. Its physical size should be the same as that of the battery which it is replacing.

When hooking up the battery cables, be careful to observe proper polarity. The positive (hot) cable should be connected to the positive (+) terminal of the battery and the negative cable (ground) should be connected to the negative (−) terminal.

Lubrication

OIL AND FUEL RECOMMENDATIONS

The engine in the Chevrolet LUV pickup truck is designed to operate on regular gasoline of at least 91 octane by the Research Method. If the vehicle is being used for heavy-duty service, do not use lead-free gas unless equipped with a catalytic converter. If the LUV is being used in light-duty service, a tank of lead-free gas can be used without any problems. If your vehicle pings or knocks, use a higher octane fuel or retard the timing of the engine, but not more than 3° from the setting required for proper operation. This is only recommended for an emergency situation until you can get some higher octane fuel. A

Ambient Temperature	Multiviscosity Engine Oil
Below −10° F to +10° F	5W-20
+10° F to +80° F	20W-20
−20° F to +90° F	10W-30
−20° F to Above +90° F	10W-40
+10° F to Above +90° F	20W-40

	Single-Viscosity Engine Oil
Below −10° F	5W*
Between −10° F and +10° F	10W*
Between +10° F and +32° F	20W
Between +32° F and +50° F	20
Between +32° F and +90° F	30
Above +80° F	40

* A sustained speed of 60 mph or higher should not be maintained with SAE5W, 5W-20 or 10W oil in the engine because the engine will force oil past the piston rings and burn it in the combustion chamber. Oil consumption will be higher than normal.

little knocking at low-speeds in an emergency is acceptable, but continued knock at high-speeds is damaging to the engine.

Many factors help to determine the proper oil for your LUV. The big question is what viscosity to use and when. The whole question of viscosity revolves around the lowest anticipated ambient temperatures to be encountered before your next oil change. Whatever the viscosity chosen, choose only those oils with an SE rating. Multiviscosity oils are recommended over single viscosity oils because of the wider range of acceptable temperatures and driving conditions the former is able to withstand.

OIL CHANGES

Engine

Change the engine oil at the intervals specified in the level checks section. Change the oil and filter after the first 600 miles only.

Change the oil as follows:

1. Drive the vehicle for 15 minutes at expressway speeds or the equivalent of city driving to make sure that the oil is at its normal operating temperature. Hot oil will hold more impurities in suspension and will flow better, allowing it to remove more oil and dirt.

2. Park on a level surface.

3. Place a pan of adequate capacity under the oil pan drain.

4. Loosen the drain plug with the proper size wrench. Unscrew the plug with your fingers, using a rag to shield your fingers from the heat. Push in on the plug as you unscrew it so you can feel when all of the screw threads are out of the hole. You can then remove the plug quickly with a minimum amount of oil running down your arm and you will also have the plug in your hand and not in the bottom of a pan of hot oil. Be careful of the oil. If it is at operating temperatures it is hot enough to burn you or at least make you uncomfortable.

5. After the oil has drained fully, remove the container used to catch the oil and reinstall the drain plug and gasket and tighten it. Don't strip the threads by tightening the plug too much.

6. Add the proper amount of new oil

through the oil filler on the top of the valve cover.

7. Check to make sure that the oil level registers Full on the oil dipstick and start the engine. Watch the oil gauge to make sure that the oil pressure comes up to the proper level. Check for leaks while the engine is running (oil filter).

8. Stop the engine, check the oil level and adjust if necessary and replace the oil filler cap.

Transmission

1. Park the truck on a level surface and put on the parking brake.

2. Remove the oil filler (upper) plug.

3. Place a container, of a large enough capacity to catch all of the oil, under the drain (lower) plug. Use the proper size wrench to loosen the drain plug slowly, while maintaining a slight upward force to keep the oil from running out. Once the plug is removed, allow all of the oil to drain from the transmission.

4. Clean and install the magnetic drain plug and its gasket, if so equipped.

5. Fill the transmission to capacity. (See the "Capacities" chart.) Use engine oil of the correct viscosity for the existing ambient temperatures as given below:

SAE 10W–30, below 50° F
SAE 40, above 50°F
SAE 30, between 0°F and 90°F

Be sure that the oil level reaches the bottom of the filler plug.

6. Install the filler plug.

Rear Axle

1. With the vehicle resting on a level surface, and a drain pan large enough to hold all of the differential oil placed under the drain hole, remove the drain plug.

2. Allow the lubricant to drain completely.

3. Install the drain plug. Tighten it so that it will not leak, but do not over-tighten.

4. Refill the axle housing with lubricant to the proper level.

5. Install the filler plug.

OIL FILTER CHANGES

The manufacturer recommends that the oil filter be changed every other oil change. Of course, it wouldn't hurt to change the filter every time the oil is changed. After all, by leaving the filter on until the next oil change you are allowing about one quart of dirty, thinned out oil to remain in the engine. The oil filter is located on the right-side of the engine and is removed from above the engine compartment.

Change the oil filter as follows:

1. Drain the oil from the crankcase. Replace the drain plug.

2. Using an oil filter wrench, loosen the oil filter from the oil pump mounting boss. Make sure that you have a container of some sort under the filter in order to catch the oil draining out of the filter.

3. Remove the old filter.

4. Coat the rubber sealing gasket on the new filter with engine oil and install it. Turn the filter only ¾ of a turn after the rubber sealing gasket comes in contact with the mounting boss.

5. Fill the crankcase with oil.

CHASSIS GREASING

It is recommended that the LUV be greased every 6,000 miles or 4 months, whichever comes first. More often if the truck is operated under heavy-duty conditions, or in dusty areas. If the vehicle is driven through deep water for a long period of time, it should be greased as soon as possible.

WHEEL BEARINGS

The front wheel bearings should be repacked every 24,000 miles or once every 2 years, whichever comes first.

Before handling the bearings there are a few things that you should remember:

Remember to DO the following:

1. Remove all outside dirt from the housing before exposing the bearing.

2. Treat a used bearing as gently as you would a new one.

3. Work with clean tools in clean surroundings.

4. Use clean, dry canvas gloves, or at least clean, dry hands.

5. Clean solvents and flushing fluids are a must.

6. Use clean paper when laying out the bearings to dry.

7. Protect disassembled bearings from rust and dirt. Cover them up.

8. Use clean rags to wipe bearings.

9. Keep the bearings in oil-proof paper when they are to be stored or are not in use.

10. Clean the inside of the housing before replacing the bearing.

Do NOT do the following:

1. Don't work in dirty surroundings.

2. Don't use dirty, chipped, or damaged tools.

3. Try not to work on wooden work benches or use wooden mallets.

4. Don't handle bearings with dirty or moist hands.

5. Do not use gasoline for cleaning; use a safe solvent.

6. Do not spin-dry bearings with compressed air. They will be damaged.

7. Do not spin unclean bearings.

8. Avoid using cotton waste or dirty cloths to wipe bearings.

9. Try not to scratch or nick bearing surfaces.

10. Do not allow the bearing to come in contact with dirt or rust at any time.

Removal

1. Raise the front of the truck and support it securely with jackstands.

2. Remove the wheel/tire assembly.

3. Remove the hub grease cap with a large pair of pliers. Straighten and remove the cotter pin. Discard the cotter pin.

4. Remove the spindle nut retainer and unscrew the spindle nut and remove the washer.

5. Move the hub slightly from side-to-side to unseat the outer bearing. Lift the outer bearing from the hub.

6. Carefully slide the hub off the spindle.

7. From the inner side of the hub, remove the inner grease seal and lift the inner bearing from the hub. Discard the grease seal.

Cleaning, Inspection, and Packing

Place all of the bearings, nuts, washers, and dust caps in a container of solvent. Cleanliness is basic to wheel bearing maintenance. Use a soft brush to thoroughly clean each part. Make sure that every bit of dirt and grease is rinsed off, then place each cleaned part on an absorbent cloth and let them dry completely.

Inspect the bearings for pitting, flat spots, rust, and rough areas. Check the races on the hub and the spindle for the same defects and rub them clean with a rag that has been soaked in solvent. If the races show hairline cracks or worn, shiny areas, they must be replaced with new parts. Replacement seals, bearings, and other required parts can be bought at an auto parts store. The old parts that are to be replaced should be taken along to be compared with the replacement parts to ensure a perfect match.

Pack the wheel bearings with grease. There are special devices made for the specific purpose of greasing bearings, but, if one is not available, pack the wheel bearings by hand. Put a large dab of grease in the palm of your hand and push the bearing through it with a sliding motion. The grease must be forced through the side of the bearing and in between each roller. Continue until the grease begins to ooze out the other side and through the gaps between the rollers; the bearing must be completely packed with grease.

Installation

1. Install the inner wheel bearing in the reverse manner of removal, using a new grease seal.

2. Carefully mount the hub onto the spindle.

3. Position the outer bearing onto the spindle, sliding it into position in the hub.

4. Install the flat washer and the spindle nut.

5. Adjust the bearing preload in the following manner:

a. While rotating the wheel, tighten the spindle nut to 22 ft lbs of torque to seat the bearings.

b. Turn the hub 2–3 turns and loosen the nut just enough so that it can be turned with your fingers.

c. Turn the nut all the way in with your fingers and check to be sure that the hub has no free-play by trying to move it from side-to-side.

NOTE: *Turning resistance measured with a spring scale hooked to a wheel mounting stud should be 1.1–2.6 lbs when the hub begins to rotate.*

6. Install the spindle nut retainer. Insert a new cotter pin and bend the ends against the nut. Cut off the extra

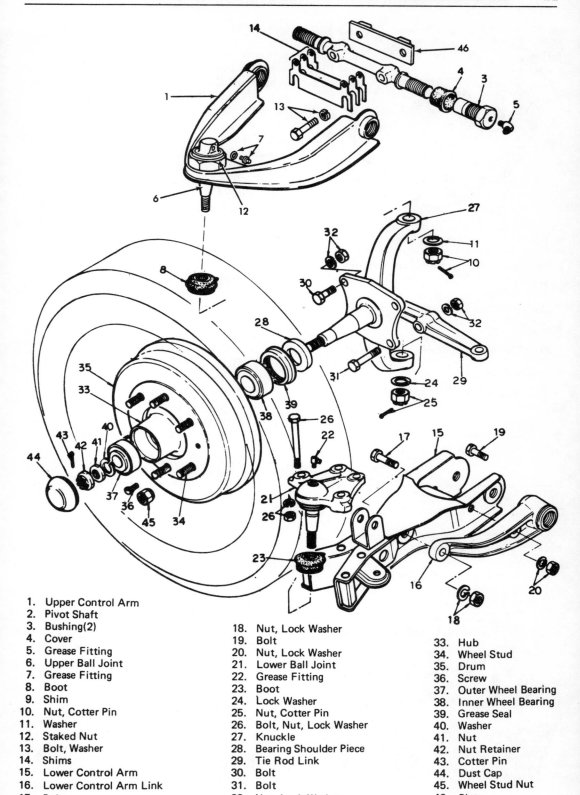

1. Upper Control Arm
2. Pivot Shaft
3. Bushing(2)
4. Cover
5. Grease Fitting
6. Upper Ball Joint
7. Grease Fitting
8. Boot
9. Shim
10. Nut, Cotter Pin
11. Washer
12. Staked Nut
13. Bolt, Washer
14. Shims
15. Lower Control Arm
16. Lower Control Arm Link
17. Bolt
18. Nut, Lock Washer
19. Bolt
20. Nut, Lock Washer
21. Lower Ball Joint
22. Grease Fitting
23. Boot
24. Lock Washer
25. Nut, Cotter Pin
26. Bolt, Nut, Lock Washer
27. Knuckle
28. Bearing Shoulder Piece
29. Tie Rod Link
30. Bolt
31. Bolt
32. Nut, Lock Washer
33. Hub
34. Wheel Stud
35. Drum
36. Screw
37. Outer Wheel Bearing
38. Inner Wheel Bearing
39. Grease Seal
40. Washer
41. Nut
42. Nut Retainer
43. Cotter Pin
44. Dust Cap
45. Wheel Stud Nut
46. Plate

An exploded view of the front hub, spindle, and suspension

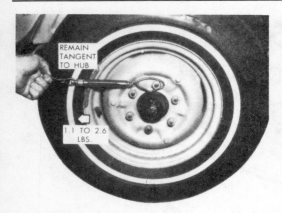

Measuring the turning resistance with a spring scale to determine the wheel bearing adjustment

length to ensure that the ends will not interfere with the dust cap.

7. Install the dust cap, wheel/tire assembly and the hub cap. Tighten the lug nuts to 65 ft lbs.

8. Perform the above operation for both the front wheels.

Bearing Diagnosis

This section will help in the diagnosis of bearing failure. Such a diagnosis can be helpful in determining the cause of axle failure. The illustrations will help to take some of the guesswork out of deciding when to use an old bearing and when to replace it with a new one.

When disassembling an axle, the general condition of all bearings should be noted and classified where possible. Proper recognition of the cause will help in correcting the problem and avoiding a repetition of the failure.

Some of the common causes of bearing failure are:

a. Abuse during assembly or disassembly;

b. Improper assembly methods;

c. Improper or inadequate lubrication;

d. Bearing contact with dirt or water;

e. Wear caused by dirt or metal chips;

f. Corrosion or rust;

g. Seizing due to overloading;

h. Overheating;

i. Frettage of the bearing seats;

j. Brinelling from impact or shock loading;

k. Manufacturing defects;

l. Pitting due to fatigue.

To avoid damage to the bearing from improper handling, it is best to treat a

Bearing Failure Chart

General Wear

Cause	*Serviceability*
Wear on races and rollers caused by fine abrasives	Clean all parts and check seals. Install new bearing if old one is rough or noisy.

Normal wear pattern (© Chevrolet Div. G.M. Corp.)   Step wear (© Chevrolet Div. G.M. Corp.)

Step Wear

Cause	Serviceability
Wear pattern on roller ends caused by fine abrasives	Clean all parts and check seals. Install new bearings if old one is rough or noisy.

Indentations

Cause	Serviceability
Surface depressions on races and rollers caused by hard foreign particles	Clean all parts and check seals. Install new bearing if old one is rough or noisy.

Indentations (Chevrolet Div. G.M. Corp.)

Galling (© Chevrolet Div. G.M. Corp.)

Galling

Cause	Serviceability
Metal smears on roller ends due to overheating from improper lubricant or overloading	Install a new bearing. Check seals and use proper lubricant.

Etching (© Chevrolet Div. G.M. Corp.)

Cage wear (© Chevrolet Div. G.M. Corp.)

Etching

Cause	Serviceability
Bearing surfaces appear gray or gray-black with related etching	Install new bearing and check seals. Use proper lubricant.

Cage Wear

Cause	Serviceability
Wear around outside diameter of cage and rollers caused by foreign material and poor lubrication	Clean all parts, check seals, and install new bearing.

Fatigue Spalling

Cause	Serviceability
Flaking of surface metal due to fatigue	Clean all parts and install new bearing.

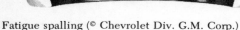

Fatigue spalling (© Chevrolet Div. G.M. Corp.)   Heat discoloration (© Chevrolet Div. G.M. Corp.)

Heat Discoloration

Cause	Serviceability
Discoloration from faint yellow to dark blue due to overload or lubricant breakdown. Softening of races or rollers also	Check for softening of parts by drawing a file over suspected area. The file will glide easily over hard metal, but will cut soft metal. If overheating is evident, install new bearings. Check seals and other parts.

Stain Discoloration

Cause	Serviceability
Stain discoloration ranging from light brown to black, caused by lubricant breakdown or moisture	Reuse bearings if stains can be removed by light polishing and no overheating exists. Check seals.

Stain discoloration (© Chevrolet Div. G.M. Corp.)   Brinelling (© Chevrolet Div. G.M. Corp.)

Brinelling

Cause	Serviceability
Surface indentations in race caused by rollers under impact load or vibration while the bearing is not rotating	If the old bearing is rough or noisy, install a new bearing.

Bent Cage

Cause	Serviceability
Improper handling	Install a new bearing.

Bent cage (© Chevrolet Div. G.M. Corp.)

Misalignment

Cause	Serviceability
Outer race misaligned as shown	Install a new bearing and be sure races and bearing are properly seated.

Misalignment (© Chevrolet Div. G.M. Corp.)

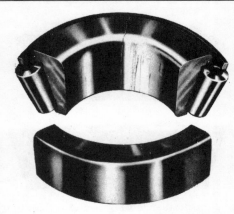

Cracked inner race (© Chevrolet Div. G.M. Corp.)

Cracked Inner Race

Cause	Serviceability
Crack due to improper fit, cocked bearing, or poor bearing seats	Install a new bearing and be sure it is seated properly.

Frettage

Cause	Serviceability
Corrosion due to small movement of parts with no lubrication	Clean parts and check seals. Install a new bearing and be sure of proper lubrication.

Frettage (© Chevrolet Div. G.M. Corp.)

Smears (© Chevrolet Div. G.M. Corp.)

Smears

Cause	Serviceability
Metal smears due to slippage caused by poor fit, improper lubrication, overloading, or handling damage	Clean parts, install new bearing, and check for proper fit and lubrication.

used bearing the same as a new bearing. Always work in a clean area with clean tools. Remove all outside dirt from the housing before exposing a bearing and clean all bearing seats before installing a bearing.

CAUTION: *Never spin a bearing, either by hand or with compressed air. This will lead to almost certain bearing failure.*

Pushing, Towing, and Jump Starting

To push-start your vehicle, follow the procedures below. Check to make sure that the bumpers of both vehicles are aligned so neither will be damaged. Be sure that all electrical system components are turned off (headlights, heater, blower, etc.). Turn on the ignition switch. Place the shift lever in Third or Fourth and push in the clutch pedal. At about 15 mph, signal the driver of the pushing vehicle to fall back, depress the accelerator pedal, and release the clutch pedal slowly. The engine should start.

When you are doing the pushing or pulling, make sure that the two bumpers match so you won't damage the vehicle you are to push. Another good idea is to put an old tire in between the two vehicles. If the bumpers don't match, perhaps you should tow the other vehicle. If the other vehicle is just stuck, use First gear to slowly push it out. Tell the driver of the other vehicle to go slowly too. Try

to keep your vehicle right up against the other vehicle while you are pushing. If the two vehicles do separate, stop and start over again instead of trying to catch up and ramming the other vehicle. Also try, as much as possible, to avoid riding or slipping the clutch. When the other

Raising a rear wheel with the scissors jack placed under the frame rail

Raising the front of the truck with a hydraulic floor jack. Note the block of wood placed between the jack lifting platform and the crossmember to prevent damage

Raising a front wheel with the scissors jack placed under the frame rail

Raising the rear of the truck with a hydraulic floor jack placed under the rear axle housing

vehicle gains enough traction, it should pull away from your vehicle.

If you have to tow the other vehicle, make sure that the tow chain or rope is sufficiently long and strong, and that it is attached securely to both vehicles at a strong place. Attach the chain at a point on the frame or as close to it as possible. Once again, go slowly and tell the other driver to do the same. Warn the other driver not to allow too much slack in the line when he gains traction and can move under his own power. Otherwise he may run over the tow line and damage both vehicles. If your LUV has to be towed by a tow truck, it can be towed forward for any distance just as long as it is done fairly slowly. If your LUV has to be towed for any great distance, tow it backward, or remove the drive shaft to prevent the transmission from rotating.

Jacking and Hoisting

The LUV may be jacked at points under the frame or under the rear axle housing.

2 · Tune-Up and Troubleshooting

Tune-Up Procedures

NOTE: *The procedures found in this section are specific ones pertaining to the LUV in particular. General procedures are outlined in the "Tune-Up" section following this section.*

SPARK PLUGS

Spark plugs ignite the air and fuel mixture in the cylinder as the piston reaches the top of the compression stroke. The controlled explosion that results forces the piston down, turning the crankshaft and the rest of the drive train.

The average life of a spark plug is 12,000 miles. This is, however, dependent on a number of factors: the mechanical condition of the engine; the type of fuel; driving conditions; and the driver.

When you remove the spark plugs, check their condition. They are a good indicator of the condition of the engine. It is a good idea to remove the spark plugs at regular intervals, such as every 3,000 or 4,000 miles, just so you can keep an eye on the mechanical state of your engine.

A small deposit of light tan or gray material on a spark plug that has been used for any period of time is to be considered normal. Any other color, or abnormal amounts of deposit, indicate that there is something amiss in the engine.

The gap between the center electrode and the side or ground electrode can be expected to increase not more than 0.001 in. every 1,000 miles under normal conditions.

When a spark plug is functioning normally or, more accurately, when the plug is installed in an engine that is functioning properly, the plugs can be taken out, cleaned, regapped, and reinstalled in the engine without doing the engine any harm.

When, and if, a plug fouls and begins to misfire, you will have to investigate, correct the cause of the fouling, and either clean or replace the plug.

There are several reasons why a spark plug will foul and you can learn which is at fault by just looking at the plug. A few of the most common reasons for plug fouling, and a description of the fouled plug's appearance, is listed in the "Troubleshooting" section, which also offers solutions to the problems.

Removal

1. Number the wires so you won't cross them when you replace them.

2. Remove the wire from the end of the spark plug by grasping the wire by the rubber boot. If the boot sticks to the plug, remove it by twisting and pulling

Tune-up Specifications

Year	Engine No. Cyl Displacement cu in. (cc)	Spark Plugs Type	Gap (in.)	Distributor Point Dwell (deg)	Point Gap (in.)	Ignition Timing (deg) MT	AT	Intake Valve Opens (deg)	Fuel Pump Pressure (psi)	Compression Pressure (psi)	Idle Speed (rpm) MT	AT	Valve Clearance (in.) In	Ex
1972–74	4-110.8 (1817)	BP-6ES④	0.030④	49–55	②	③	—	31	3–4.5	163	⑤	—	0.004	0.006
1975	4-110.8 (1817)	BP-6ES④	0.030④	①	①	①	—	31	3–4.5	163	①	—	①	①

① See tune-up sticker in the engine compartment
② On 1972 and 1973 dual point distributor: Retarded points—0.016–0.024 in.; Advanced points—0.018–0.022 in. On 1974 single point distributor: 0.016–0.024 in.
③ 8°B @ 700 rpm—1972–73; 12°B @ 700 rpm—1974
④ Or AC-R42T with 0.035 in. gap—1972, or AC-44XLS with 0.035 in. gap—1974
⑤ 1,000 rpm—1972; 700 rpm—1973; 700 rpm w/o AC and 900 rpm w/AC—1974
— Not applicable

NOTE: *If the figures in this chart vary from the figures on the tune-up sticker in the engine compartment, use the figures on the sticker.*

at the same time. Do not pull the wire itself or you will most certainly damage the delicate carbon core.

3. Use a ¹³/₁₆ in. spark plug socket to loosen all of the plugs about two turns.

4. If compressed air is available, blow off the area around the spark plug holes. Otherwise, use a rag or a brush to clean the area. Be careful not to allow any foreign material to drop into the spark plug holes.

5. Remove the plugs by unscrewing them the rest of the way from the engine.

Inspection

Check the plugs for deposits and wear. If they are not going to be replaced, clean the plugs thoroughly. Remember that any kind of deposit will decrease the efficiency of the plug. Plugs can be cleaned on a spark plug cleaning machine, which can sometimes be found in service stations, or you can do an acceptable job of cleaning with a stiff brush.

Check spark plug gap before installation. The ground electrode must be parallel to the center electrode and the specified size wire gauge should pass through the gap with a slight drag. If the electrodes are worn, it is possible to file them level.

Installation

1. Insert the plugs in the spark plug hole and tighten them hand-tight. Take care not to cross-thread them.

2. Tighten the plugs to 18–25 ft lbs.

3. Install the spark plug wires on their plugs. Make sure that each wire is firmly connected to each plug.

Measuring the spark plug electrode gap

BREAKER POINTS

The points function as a circuit breaker for the primary circuit of the ignition system. The ignition coil must boost the 12 volts of electrical pressure supplied by the battery to as much as 25,000 volts in order to fire the plugs. To do this, the coil depends on the points and the condenser to make a clean break in the primary circuit.

The coil has both primary and secondary circuits. When the ignition is turned on, the battery supplies voltage through the coil and onto the points. The points are connected to ground, completing the primary circuit. As the current passes through the coil, a magnetic field is created in the iron center core of the coil. As the cam in the distributor turns, the points open and the primary circuit collapses. The magnetic field in the primary circuit of the coil also collapses and cuts through the secondary circuit windings around the iron core. Because of the scientific phenomenon called "electromagnetic induction," the battery voltage is increased to a level sufficient to fire the spark plugs.

When the points open, the electrical charge in the primary circuit jumps the gap created between the two open contacts of the points. If this electrical charge were not transferred elsewhere, the metal contacts of the points would melt and the gap between the points would start to change rapidly. If this gap is not maintained, the points will not break the primary circuit. If the primary circuit is not broken, the secondary circuit will not have enough voltage to fire the spark plugs.

It is interesting to note that the above cycle must be completed by the ignition system every time a spark plug fires. In a 4 cycle engine such as the LUV's 4 cylinder engine, all of the spark plugs fire once for every two revolutions of the crankshaft. That means that in one revolution, 2 spark plugs fire. So, when the engine is at an idle speed of 800 rpm, the points are opening and closing 1,600 times a minute. Just think how many

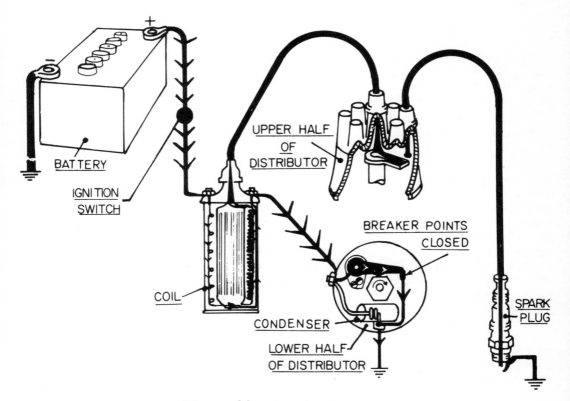

Diagram of the primary ignition circuit

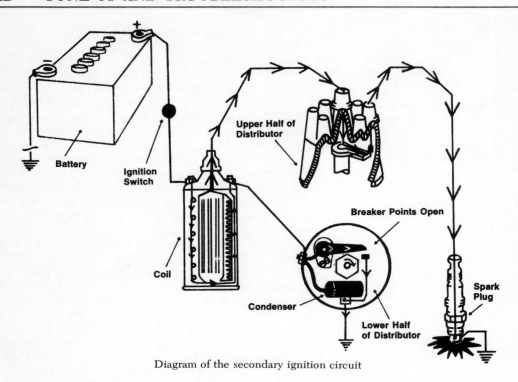

Diagram of the secondary ignition circuit

times they are opening and closing at 60 mph!

CONDENSER

The function of the condenser is to absorb excessive voltage from the points when they open and thus prevent the points from becoming pitted or burned.

BREAKER POINT DWELL

There are two ways to check the breaker point gap: It can be done with a feeler gauge or a dwell meter. Either way you set the points, you are basically adjusting the amount of time that the points remain open. The time is measured in degrees of distributor rotation. When you measure the gap between the breaker points with a feeler gauge, you are setting the maximum amount the points will open when the rubbing block on the points is on a high point of the distributor cam. When you adjust the points with a dwell meter, you are adjusting the number of degrees that the points will remain closed before they start to open as a high point of the distributor cam approaches the rubbing block of the points.

When you replace a set of points,

always replace the condenser at the same time.

When you change the point gap or dwell, you will also have changed the ignition timing. So, if the point gap or dwell is changed, the ignition timing must be adjusted also.

NOTE: *See Chapter 4, "Fuel System and Emission Controls" for an additional explanation of the dual point distributor and how it works.*

Inspection of the Points

1. Disconnect the high-tension wire from the top of the distributor and the coil.

2. Remove the distributor cap by prying off the spring clips on the sides of the cap.

3. Remove the rotor from the distributor shaft by pulling it straight up. Examine the condition of the rotor. If it is cracked or the metal tip is excessively worn or burned, it should be replaced. Clean the metal tip with fine emery paper.

4. Pry open the contacts of the points with a screwdriver and check the condition of the contacts. If they are excessively worn, burned or pitted, they should be replaced.

5. If the points are in good condition, adjust them and replace the rotor and the distributor cap. If the points need to be replaced, follow the replacement procedure given below.

Replacement of the Breaker Points and Condenser

NOTE: *Dual point distributors used in 1972–73 LUVs are serviced in a similar manner as single point units as far as replacement of the breaker points is concerned.*

1. Remove the coil high-tension wire from top of the distributor cap. Remove the distributor cap from the distributor and place it out of the way. Remove the rotor from the distributor shaft.

2. Loosen the screw that holds the condenser lead to the body of the breaker points and remove the condenser lead from the points.

3. Remove the screw that holds and grounds the condenser to the distributor body. Remove the condenser from the distributor and discard it.

4. Remove the points assembly attaching screws and adjustment lockscrews. A screwdriver with a holding mechanism will come in handy here, so that you don't drop a screw into the distributor and have to remove the entire distributor to retrieve it.

5. Remove the points by lifting them straight up and off the locating dowel on the plate. Wipe off the cam and apply new cam lubricant. Discard the old set of points.

6. Slip the new set of points onto the locating dowel and install the screws that hold the assembly onto the plate. Do not tighten them all the way.

7. Attach the new condenser to the plate with the ground screw.

8. Attach the condenser lead to the points at the proper place.

9. Apply a small amount of cam lubricant to the shaft where the rubbing block of the points touches.

Adjustment of the Breaker Points with a Feeler Gauge

SINGLE POINT DISTRIBUTOR

1. If the contact points of the assembly are not parallel, bend the stationary contact so that they make contact across the entire surface of the contacts. Bend only the stationary bracket part of the point assembly; not the moveable contact.

2. Turn the engine until the rubbing block of the points is on one of the high points of the distributor cam. You can do this by either turning the ignition switch to the start position and releasing it quickly ("bumping" the engine) or by using a wrench on the bolt that holds the crankshaft pulley to the crankshaft.

3. Place the correct size feeler gauge between the contacts. Make sure it is parallel with the contact surfaces.

4. With your free hand, insert a screwdriver into the notch provided for adjustment or into the eccentric adjusting screw, then twist the screwdriver to either increase or decrease the gap to the proper setting.

5. Tighten the adjustment lockscrew and recheck the contact gap to make sure that it didn't change when the lockscrew was tightened.

6. Replace the rotor and distributor cap, and the high-tension wire that connects the top of the distributor and the coil. Make sure that the rotor is firmly seated all the way onto the distributor shaft and that the tab of the rotor is aligned with notch in the shaft. Align the tab in the base of the distributor cap with the notch in the distributor body. Make sure that the cap is firmly seated on the distributor and that the retainer springs are in place. Make sure that the end of the high-tension wire is firmly placed in the top of the distributor and the coil.

DUAL POINT DISTRIBUTOR

The two sets of breaker points are adjusted with a feeler gauge in the same manner as those in a single point distributor. Check the "Tune-Up Specifications" chart for the correct setting for either set of points; they are not the same.

Adjustment of the Breaker Points with a Dwell Meter

SINGLE POINT DISTRIBUTOR

1. Adjust the points with a feeler gauge as previously described.

2. Connect the dwell meter to the ignition circuit as according to the manu-

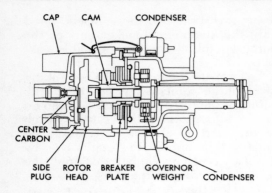

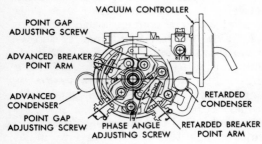

Dual point distributor

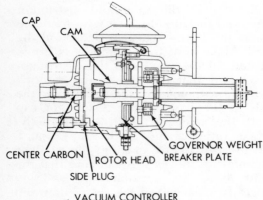

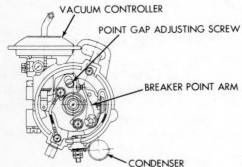

Single point distributor

facturer's instructions. One lead of the meter is connected to a ground and the other lead is connected to the distributor post on the coil. An adapter is usually provided for this purpose.

3. If the dwell meter has a set line on it, adjust the meter to zero the indicator.

4. Start the engine.

NOTE: *Be careful when working on any vehicle while the engine is running. Make sure that the transmission is in Neutral and that the parking brake is applied. Keep hands, clothing, tools and the wires of the test instruments clear of the rotating fan blades.*

5. Observe the reading on the dwell meter. If the reading is within the specified range, turn off the engine and remove the dwell meter.

NOTE: *If the meter does not have a scale for 4 cylinder engines, multiply the 8 cylinder reading by two.*

6. If the reading is above the specified range, the breaker point gap is too small. If the reading is below the specified range, the gap is too large. In either case, the engine must be stopped and the gap adjusted in the manner previously covered.

After making the adjustment, start the engine and check the reading on the dwell meter. When the correct reading is obtained, disconnect the dwell meter.

7. Check the adjustment of the ignition timing.

Dual Point Distributor

The breaker point dwell is set with a dwell meter in the same manner as for a single point distributor. However, since the retard set of points is deenergized at curb idle, it will be necessary to energize the retard set of points in order to get a reading on a dwell meter. After adjusting the dwell of the advance set of points at curb idle speed, have an assistant depress the accelerator pedal at least 7° or move the throttle linkage enough to energize the accelerator switch, opening the accelerator relay-to-distributor relay circuit, thus energizing the retard set of breaker points, and getting retard breaker point dwell reading.

IGNITION TIMING

Ignition timing is the measurement, in degrees of crankshaft rotation, of the point at which the spark plugs fire in each of the cylinders. It is measured in degrees before or after Top Dead Center (TDC) of the compression stroke. Ignition timing is controlled by turning the distributor body in the engine.

Ideally, the air/fuel mixture in the cylinder will be ignited by the spark plug just as the piston passes TDC of the compression stroke. If this happens, the piston will be beginning its downward motion of the power stroke just as the compressed and ignited air/fuel mixture starts to expand. The expansion of the air/fuel mixture then forces the piston down on the power stroke and turns the crankshaft.

Because it takes a fraction of a second for the spark plug to ignite the mixture in the cylinder, the spark plug must fire a little before the piston reaches TDC. Otherwise, the mixture will not be completely ignited as the piston passes TDC and the full power of the explosion will not be used by the engine.

The timing measurement is given in degrees of crankshaft rotation before the piston reaches TDC (BTDC). If the setting for the ignition timing is 5° BTDC, the spark plug must fire 5° before each piston reaches TDC. This only holds true, however, when the engine is at idle speed.

As the engine speed increases, the pistons go faster. The spark plugs have to ignite the fuel even sooner if it is to be completely ignited when the piston reaches TDC. To do this, the distributor has a means to advance the timing of the spark as the engine speed increases. This is accomplished by centrifugal weights within the distributor and a vacuum diaphragm, mounted on the side of the distributor. It is necessary to disconnect the vacuum line from the diaphragm when the igniton timing is being set.

If the ignition is set too far advanced (BTDC), the ignition and expansion of the fuel in the cylinder will occur too soon and tend to force the piston down while it is still traveling up. This causes engine ping. If the ignition spark is set too far retarded, after TDC (ATDC), the piston will have already passed TDC and started on its way down when the fuel is ignited. This will cause the piston to be forced down for only a portion of its travel. This will result in poor engine performance and lack of power.

The timing is best checked with a timing light. This device is connected in series with the No. 1 spark plug. The current which fires the spark plug also causes the timing light to flash.

The timing marks are located at the front crankshaft pulley and consist of a pointer attached to the engine block and graduations on the crankshaft pulley.

When the engine is running, the timing light is aimed at the marks on the flywheel pulley and the pointer.

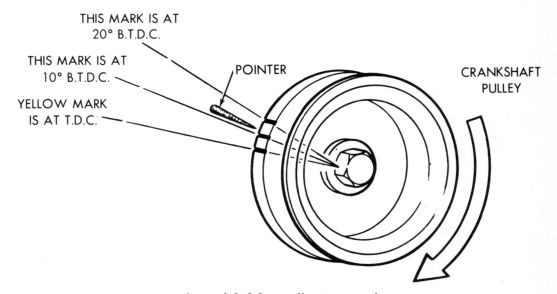

The crankshaft front pulley timing marks

Ignition Timing Adjustment

1. Set the dwell of the breaker points to the proper specification.

2. Locate the timing marks on the crankshaft pulley and the front of the engine.

3. Clean off the timing marks, so that you can see them.

4. Use chalk or white paint to color the mark on the crankshaft pulley that will indicate the correct timing, when aligned with the pointer. It is also helpful to mark the tip of the pointer with a small dab of color.

5. Attach a tachometer to the engine.

6. Attach a timing light to the engine, according to the manufacturer's instructions. If the timing light has three wires, one, usually green or blue, is attached to the No. 1 spark plug with an adapter. The other wires are connected to the battery. The red wire goes to the positive side of the battery and the black wire is connected to the negative terminal of the battery.

7. Disconnect the vacuum line to the distributor at the distributor and plug the vacuum line. A golf tee does a fine job.

8. Check to make sure that all of the wires clear the fan and then start the engine.

9. Adjust the idle to the correct setting.

10. Aim the timing light at the timing marks. If the marks that you put on the pulley and the engine are aligned when the light flashes, the timing is correct. Turn off the engine and remove the tachometer and the timing light. If the marks are not in alignment, proceed with the following steps.

11. Turn off the engine.

12. Loosen the distributor lockbolt just enough so that the distributor can be turned with a little effort.

13. Start the engine. Keep the wires of the timing light clear of the fan.

14. With the timing light aimed at the pulley and the marks on the engine, turn the distributor in the direction of rotor rotation to retard the spark, and in the opposite direction of rotor rotation to advance the spark. Align the marks on the pulley and the engine with the flashes of the timing light.

VALVE LASH

Valve adjustment determines how far the valves enter the cylinder and how long they stay open and closed.

If the valve clearance is too large, part of the lift of the camshaft will be used in removing the excessive clearance. Consequently, the valve will not be opening as far as it should. This condition has two effects: the valve train components will emit a tapping sound as they take up the excessive clearance and the engine will perform poorly because the valves don't open fully and allow the proper amount of gases to flow into and out of the engine.

If the valve clearance is too small, the intake valves and the exhaust valves will open too far and they will not fully seat on the cylinder head when they close. When a valve seats itself on the cylinder head, it does two things: it seals the combustion chamber so that none of the gases in the cylinder escape and it cools itself by transferring some of the heat it absorbs from the combustion in the cylinder to the cylinder head and to the engine's cooling system. If the valve clearance is too small, the engine will run poorly because of the gases escaping from the combustion chamber. The valves will also become overheated and will warp, since they cannot transfer heat unless they are touching the valve seat in the cylinder head.

NOTE: *While all valve adjustments must be made as accurately as possible, it is better to have the valve adjustment slightly loose than slightly tight, as a burned valve may result from overly tight adjustments.*

Adjustment

NOTE: *The valves are adjusted with the engine cold.*

1. Make sure that the cylinder head and camshaft retaining bolts are tightened to the proper torque.

2. Remove the camshaft carrier side cover.

3. Turn the crankshaft with a wrench on the front pulley attaching bolt or by "bumping" the engine with the starter until the No. 1 piston is at TDC of the compression stroke. You can tell when the piston is coming up on the compres-

sion stroke by removing the spark plug and placing your thumb over the hole and you will feel air being forced out of the spark plug hole past your thumb. Stop turning the crankshaft when the TDC timing mark on the crankshaft pulley is directly aligned with the timing mark pointer.

4. With the No. 1 piston at TDC of the compression stroke, check the clearance between the rocker arm and the camshaft with the proper thickness feeler gauge on Nos. 1 and 2 intake valves and Nos. 1 and 3 exhaust valves.

Adjusting the valves. The feeler gauge is placed between the rocker arm and the camshaft lobe

Number of Cylinders	1		2		3		4	
Valve Arrangement	Exh.	In.	In.	Exh.	Exh.	In.	In.	Exh.
When piston in No. 1 cylinder is held at T.D.C.	0	0	0		0			
When piston in No. 4 cylinder is held at T.D.C.				0		0	0	0

Valve adjusting sequence

5. Adjust the clearance by loosening the locknut with an open-end wrench, turning the adjusting screw with a phillips head screwdriver and retightening the locknut. The proper thickness feeler gauge should pass between the camshaft and the rocker with a slight drag when the clearance is correct.

6. Turn the crankshaft one full turn to position the No. 4 piston at TDC of its compression stroke. Adjust the remaining valves: Nos. 2 and 4 exhaust and Nos. 3 and 4 intake in the same manner as outlined in Step 5.

7. Install the camshaft carrier side-cover

CARBURETOR

This section contains only tune-up adjustment procedures for carburetors. Descriptions, adjustments, and overhaul procedures for carburetors can be found in the "Fuel System" section.

When the engine in your LUV is running, the air-fuel mixture from the carburetor is being drawn into the engine by a partial vacuum which is created by the movement of the pistons downward on the intake stroke. The amount of air-fuel mixture that enters into the engine is controlled by the throttle plate(s) in the bottom of the carburetor. When the engine is not running the throttle plate(s) is closed, completely blocking off the bottom of the carburetor from the inside of the engine. The throttle plates are connected by the throttle linkage to the accelerator pedal in the passenger compartment of the LUV. When you depress the pedal, you open the throttle plates in the carburetor to admit more air-fuel mixture to the engine.

When the engine is not running, the throttle plates are closed. When the engine is idling, it is necessary to have the throttle plates open slightly. To prevent having to hold your foot on the pedal when the engine is idling, an idle speed adjusting screw was added to the carburetor linkage.

The idle adjusting screw contacts a lever (throttle lever) on the outside of the carburetor. When the screw is turned, it either opens or closes the throttle plates of the carburetor, raising or lowering the idle speed of the engine. This screw is called the curb idle adjusting screw.

Idle Speed and Mixture Adjustment

1. Start the engine and run it until it reaches operating temperature.

2. If it hasn't already been done, check and adjust the ignition timing. After you have set the timing, turn off the engine.

3. Attach a tachometer to the engine.

4. Remove the air cleaner.

5. Start the engine and, with the

transmission in Neutral, check the idle speed on the tachometer. If the reading on the tachometer is correct, turn off the engine and remove the tachometer. If it is not correct, proceed to the following steps.

6. Turn the idle adjusting screw with a screwdriver—clockwise to increase idle speed and counterclockwise to decrease it.

7. If the vehicle is equipped with air conditioning:

a. Turn on the AC to maximum cold and high blower. Disconnect the vacuum line to the air cleaner hot air compensator and plug the inlet manifold;

b. Open the throttle approximately ⅓ and allow the throttle to close. This will allow the speed-up solenoid to reach full travel;

c. Adjust the speed-up controller adjusting screw to set the idle speed to 900 rpm;

d. Open the throttle about ⅓ and allow it to close. Read the idle rpm. If it is not at 900 rpm, repeat step c until the correct reading is obtained. Shut off the engine.

8. Turn the mixture adjusting screw all the way. Seat the needle tip *lightly* to avoid damaging the tip. Back the screw out 3½ turns.

9. Start the engine. Turn the mixture screw out until engine rpm starts to drop due to an overly rich mixture.

10. Turn the screw in past the starting point until the engine rpm starts to drop because of a too lean mixture.

11. Turn the mixture screw back out to the point midway between the two extreme positions where the engine began losing rpm to achieve the fastest and smoothest idle.

12. Adjust the curb idle speed to the proper specification.

13. Reconnect the air cleaner hot idle compensator vacuum line.

Engine Tune-Up

Engine tune-up is a procedure performed to restore engine performance, deteriorated due to normal wear and loss of adjustment. The three major areas considered in a routine tune-up are compression, ignition, and carburetion, although valve adjustment may be included.

A tune-up is performed in three steps: *analysis*, in which it is determined whether normal wear is responsible for performance loss, and which parts require replacement or service; *parts replacement or service*; and *adjustment*, in which engine adjustments are returned to original specifications. Since the advent of emission control equipment, precision adjustment has become increasingly critical, in order to maintain pollutant emission levels.

Analysis

The procedures below are used to indicate where adjustments, parts service or replacement are necessary within the realm of a normal tune-up. If, following these tests, all systems appear to be functioning properly, proceed to the Troubleshooting Section for further diagnosis.

—Remove all spark plugs, noting the cylinder in which they were installed. Remove the air cleaner, and position the throttle and choke in the full open position. Disconnect the coil high tension lead from the coil and the distributor cap. Insert a compression gauge into the spark plug port of each cylinder, in succession, and crank the engine with

Maxi. Press. Lbs. Sq. In.	Min. Press. Lbs. Sq. In.	Max. Press. Lbs. Sq. In.	Min. Press. Lbs. Sq. In.
134	101	188	141
136	102	190	142
138	104	192	144
140	105	194	145
142	107	196	147
146	110	198	148
148	111	200	150
150	113	202	151
152	114	204	153
154	115	206	154
156	117	208	156
158	118	210	157
160	120	212	158
162	121	214	160
164	123	216	162
166	124	218	163
168	126	220	165
170	127	222	166
172	129	224	168
174	131	226	169
176	132	228	171
178	133	230	172
180	135	232	174
182	136	234	175
184	138	236	177
186	140	238	178

Compression pressure limits
© Buick Div. G.M. Corp.)

the starter to obtain the highest possible reading. Record the readings, and compare the highest to the lowest on the compression pressure limit chart. If the difference exceeds the limits on the chart, or if all readings are excessively low, proceed to a wet compression check (see Troubleshooting Section).

—Evaluate the spark plugs according to the spark plug chart in the Troubleshooting Section, and proceed as indicated in the chart.

—Remove the distributor cap, and inspect it inside and out for cracks and/or carbon tracks, and inside for excessive wear or burning of the rotor contacts. If any of these faults are evident, the cap must be replaced.

—Check the breaker points for burning, pitting or wear, and the contact heel resting on the distributor cam for excessive wear. If defects are noted, replace the entire breaker point set.

—Remove and inspect the rotor. If the contacts are burned or worn, or if the rotor is excessively loose on the distributor shaft (where applicable), the rotor must be replaced.

—Inspect the spark plug leads and the coil high tension lead for cracks or brittleness. If any of the wires appear defective, the entire set should be replaced.

—Check the air filter to ensure that it is functioning properly.

Parts Replacement and Service

The determination of whether to replace or service parts is at the mechanic's discretion; however, it is suggested that any parts in questionable condition be replaced rather than reused.

—Clean and regap, or replace, the spark plugs as needed. Lightly coat the threads with engine oil and install the plugs. CAUTION: *Do not over-torque taper-seat spark plugs, or plugs being installed in aluminum cylinder heads.*

29

—If the distributor cap is to be reused, clean the inside with a dry rag, and remove corrosion from the rotor contact points with fine emery cloth. Remove the spark plug wires one by one, and clean the wire ends and the inside of the towers. If the boots are loose, they should be replaced.

If the cap is to be replaced, transfer the wires one by one, cleaning the wire ends and replacing the boots if necessary.

—If the original points are to remain in service, clean them lightly with emery cloth, lubricate the contact heel with grease specifically designed for this purpose. Rotate the crankshaft until the heel rests on a high point of the distributor cam, and adjust the point gap to specifications.

When replacing the points, remove the original points and condenser, and wipe out the inside of the distributor housing with a clean, dry rag. Lightly lubricate the contact heel and pivot point, and install the points and condenser. Rotate the crankshaft until the heel rests on a high point of the distributor cam, and adjust the point gap to specifications. NOTE: *Always replace the condenser when changing the points.*

—If the rotor is to be reused, clean the contacts with solvent. Do not alter the spring tension of the rotor center contact. Install the rotor and the distributor cap.

—Replace the coil high tension lead and/or the spark plug leads as necessary.

—Clean the carburetor using a spray solvent (e.g., Gumout Spray). Remove the varnish from the throttle bores, and clean the linkage. Disconnect and plug the fuel line, and run the engine until it runs out of fuel. Partially fill the float chamber with solvent, and reconnect the fuel line. In extreme cases, the jets can be pressure flushed by inserting a rubber plug into the float vent, running the spray nozzle through it, and spraying the solvent until it squirts out of the venturi fuel dump.

—Clean and tighten all wiring connections in the primary electrical circuit.

Additional Services

The following services *should* be performed in conjunction with a routine tune-up to ensure efficient performance.

—Inspect the battery and fill to the proper level with distilled water. Remove the cable clamps, clean clamps and posts thoroughly, coat the posts lightly with petroleum jelly, reinstall and tighten.

—Inspect all belts, replace and/or adjust as necessary.

—Test the PCV valve (if so equipped), and clean or replace as indicated. Clean all crankcase ventilation hoses, or replace if cracked or hardened.

—Adjust the valves (if necessary) to manufacturer's specifications.

Adjustments

—Connect a dwell-tachometer between the distributor primary lead and ground. Remove the distributor cap and rotor (unless equipped with Delco externally adjustable distributor). With the ignition off, crank the engine with a remote starter switch and measure the point dwell angle. Adjust the dwell angle to specifications. NOTE: *Increasing the gap decreases the dwell angle and*

vice-versa. Install the rotor and distributor cap.

—Connect a timing light according to the manufacturer's specifications. Identify the proper timing marks with chalk or paint. NOTE: *Luminescent (day-glo) paint is excellent for this purpose.* Start the engine, and run it until it reaches operating temperature. Disconnect and plug any distributor vacuum lines, and adjust idle to the speed required to adjust timing, according to specifications. Loosen the distributor clamp and adjust timing to specifications by rotating the distributor in the engine. NOTE: *To advance timing, rotate distributor opposite normal direction of rotor rotation, and vice-versa.*

—Synchronize the throttles and mixture of multiple carburetors (if so equipped) according to procedures given in the individual car sections.

—Adjust the idle speed, mixture, and idle quality, as specified in the car sections. Final idle adjustments should be made with the air cleaner installed. CAUTION: *Due to strict emission control requirements on 1969 and later models, special test equipment (CO meter, SUN Tester) may be necessary to properly adjust idle mixture to specifications.*

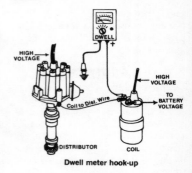

Dwell meter hook-up

Trouble-shooting

The following section is designed to aid in the rapid diagnosis of engine problems. The systematic format is used to diagnose problems ranging from engine starting difficulties to the need for engine overhaul. It is assumed that the user is equipped with basic hand tools and test equipment (tach-dwell meter, timing light, voltmeter, and ohmmeter).

Troubleshooting is divided into two sections. The first, *General Diagnosis*, is used to locate the problem area. In the second, *Specific Diagnosis*, the problem is systematically evaluated.

General Diagnosis

PROBLEM: *Symptom*	Begin diagnosis at Section Two, Number ——
Engine won't start:	
Starter doesn't turn	1.1, 2.1
Starter turns, engine doesn't	2.1
Starter turns engine very slowly	1.1, 2.4
Starter turns engine normally	3.1, 4.1
Starter turns engine very quickly	6.1
Engine fires intermittently	4.1
Engine fires consistently	5.1, 6.1
Engine runs poorly:	
Hard starting	3.1, 4.1, 5.1, 8.1
Rough idle	4.1, 5.1, 8.1
Stalling	3.1, 4.1, 5.1, 8.1
Engine dies at high speeds	4.1, 5.1
Hesitation (on acceleration from standing stop)	5.1, 8.1
Poor pickup	4.1, 5.1, 8.1
Lack of power	3.1, 4.1, 5.1, 8.1
Backfire through the carburetor	4.1, 8.1, 9.1
Backfire through the exhaust	4.1, 8.1, 9.1
Blue exhaust gases	6.1, 7.1
Black exhaust gases	5.1
Running on (after the ignition is shut off)	3.1, 8.1
Susceptible to moisture	4.1
Engine misfires under load	4.1, 7.1, 8.4, 9.1
Engine misfires at speed	4.1, 8.4
Engine misfires at idle	3.1, 4.1, 5.1, 7.1, 8.4

PROBLEM: *Symptom*	Probable Cause
Engine noises: ①	
Metallic grind while starting	Starter drive not engaging completely
Constant grind or rumble	*Starter drive not releasing, worn main bearings
Constant knock	Worn connecting rod bearings
Knock under load	Fuel octane too low, worn connecting rod bearings
Double knock	Loose piston pin
Metallic tap	*Collapsed or sticky valve lifter, excessive valve clearance, excessive end play in a rotating shaft
Scrape	*Fan belt contacting a stationary surface
Tick while starting	S.U. electric fuel pump (normal), starter brushes
Constant tick	*Generator brushes, shreaded fan belt
Squeal	*Improperly tensioned fan belt
Hiss or roar	*Steam escaping through a leak in the cooling system or the radiator overflow vent
Whistle	*Vacuum leak
Wheeze	Loose or cracked spark plug

①—It is extremely difficult to evaluate vehicle noises. While the above are general definitions of engine noises, those starred (*) should be considered as possibly originating elsewhere in the car. To aid diagnosis, the following list considers other potential sources of these sounds.

Metallic grind:
Throwout bearing; transmission gears, bearings, or synchronizers; differential bearings, gears; something metallic in contact with brake drum or disc.

Metallic tap:
U-joints; fan-to-radiator (or shroud) contact.

Scrape:
Brake shoe or pad dragging; tire to body contact; suspension contacting undercarriage or exhaust; something non-metallic contacting brake shoe or drum.

Tick:
Transmission gears; differential gears; lack of radio suppression; resonant vibration of body panels; windshield wiper motor or transmission; heater motor and blower.

Squeal:
Brake shoe or pad not fully releasing; tires (excessive wear, uneven wear, improper inflation); front or rear wheel alignment (most commonly due to improper toe-in).

Hiss or whistle:
Wind leaks (body or window); heater motor and blower fan.

Roar:
Wheel bearings; wind leaks (body and window).

Specific Diagnosis

This section is arranged so that following each test, instructions are given to proceed to another, until a problem is diagnosed.

INDEX

Group		Topic
1	*	Battery
2	*	Cranking system
3	*	Primary electrical system
4	*	Secondary electrical system
5	*	Fuel system
6	*	Engine compression
7	**	Engine vacuum
8	**	Secondary electrical system
9	**	Valve train
10	**	Exhaust system
11	**	Cooling system
12	**	Engine lubrication

*—The engine need not be running.
**—The engine must be running.

SAMPLE SECTION

Test and Procedure	Results and Indications	Proceed to
4.1—Check for spark: Hold each spark plug wire approximately ¼″ from ground with gloves or a heavy, dry rag. Crank the engine and observe the spark.	→ If no spark is evident:	→ 4.2
	→ If spark is good in some cases:	→ 4.3
	→ If spark is good in all cases:	→ 4.6

DIAGNOSIS

1.1—Inspect the battery visually for case condition (corrosion, cracks) and water level.	If case is cracked, replace battery:	1.4
	If the case is intact, remove corrosion with a solution of baking soda and water (CAUTION: *do not get the solution into the battery*), and fill with water:	1.2

1.2—Check the battery cable connections: Insert a screwdriver between the battery post and the cable clamp. Turn the headlights on high beam, and observe them as the screwdriver is gently twisted to ensure good metal to metal contact.	If the lights brighten, remove and clean the clamp and post; coat the post with petroleum jelly, install and tighten the clamp:	1.4
	If no improvement is noted:	1.3

Testing battery cable connections using a screwdriver

1.3—Test the state of charge of the battery using an individual cell tester or hydrometer.

Spec. Grav. Reading	Charged Condition
1.260-1.280	Fully Charged
1.230-1.250	Three Quarter Charged
1.200-1.220	One Half Charged
1.170-1.190	One Quarter Charged
1.140-1.160	Just About Flat
1.110-1.130	All The Way Down

State of battery charge

Electrolyte temperature (°F)	Specific gravity correction	
+ 120	+.016	
+ 100	+.012 +.008	ADD to reading
	+.004	
+ 80	no correction	
+ 60	−.004 −.008	
+ 40	−.012 −.016	
+ 20	−.020 −.024	SUBTRACT from reading
0	−.028 −.032	
− 20	−.036 −.040	

The effect of temperature on the specific gravity of battery electrolyte

If indicated, charge the battery. NOTE: *If no obvious reason exists for the low state of charge (i.e., battery age, prolonged storage), the charging system should be tested:* 1.4

Test and Procedure	*Results and Indications*	*Proceed to*
1.4—Visually inspect battery cables for cracking, bad connection to ground, or bad connection to starter.	If necessary, tighten connections or replace the cables:	2.1

Tests in Group 2 are performed with coil high tension lead disconnected to prevent accidental starting.

Test and Procedure	*Results and Indications*	*Proceed to*
2.1—Test the starter motor and solenoid: Connect a jumper from the battery post of the solenoid (or relay) to the starter post of the solenoid (or relay).	If starter turns the engine normally:	2.2
	If the starter buzzes, or turns the engine very slowly:	2.4
	If no response, replace the solenoid (or relay).	3.1
	If the starter turns, but the engine doesn't, ensure that the flywheel ring gear is intact. If the gear is undamaged, replace the starter drive.	3.1
2.2—Determine whether ignition override switches are functioning properly (clutch start switch, neutral safety switch), by connecting a jumper across the switch(es), and turning the ignition switch to "start".	If starter operates, adjust or replace switch:	3.1
	If the starter doesn't operate:	2.3
2.3—Check the ignition switch "start" position: Connect a 12V test lamp between the starter post of the solenoid (or relay) and ground. Turn the ignition switch to the "start" position, and jiggle the key.	If the lamp doesn't light when the switch is turned, check the ignition switch for loose connections, cracked insulation, or broken wires. Repair or replace as necessary:	3.1
	If the lamp flickers when the key is jiggled, replace the ignition switch.	3.3

Checking the ignition switch "start" position

Test and Procedure	*Results and Indications*	*Proceed to*
2.4—Remove and bench test the starter, according to specifications in the car section.	If the starter does not meet specifications, repair or replace as needed:	3.1
	If the starter is operating properly:	2.5
2.5—Determine whether the engine can turn freely: Remove the spark plugs, and check for water in the cylinders. Check for water on the dipstick, or oil in the radiator. Attempt to turn the engine using an 18″ flex drive and socket on the crankshaft pulley nut or bolt.	If the engine will turn freely only with the spark plugs out, and hydrostatic lock (water in the cylinders) is ruled out, check valve timing:	9.2
	If engine will not turn freely, and it is known that the clutch and transmission are free, the engine must be disassembled for further evaluation:	Next Chapter

Tests and Procedures	Results and Indications	Proceed to
3.1—Check the ignition switch "on" position: Connect a jumper wire between the distributor side of the coil and ground, and a 12V test lamp between the switch side of the coil and ground. Remove the high tension lead from the coil. Turn the ignition switch on and jiggle the key.	If the lamp lights:	3.2
	If the lamp flickers when the key is jiggled, replace the ignition switch:	3.3
	If the lamp doesn't light, check for loose or open connections. If none are found, remove the ignition switch and check for continuity. If the switch is faulty, replace it:	3.3

Checking the ignition switch "on" position

3.2—Check the ballast resistor or resistance wire for an open circuit, using an ohmmeter.	Replace the resistor or the resistance wire if the resistance is zero.	3.3
3.3—Visually inspect the breaker points for burning, pitting, or excessive wear. Gray coloring of the point contact surfaces is normal. Rotate the crankshaft until the contact heel rests on a high point of the distributor cam, and adjust the point gap to specifications.	If the breaker points are intact, clean the contact surfaces with fine emery cloth, and adjust the point gap to specifications. If pitted or worn, replace the points and condenser, and adjust the gap to specifications: NOTE: *Always lubricate the distributor cam according to manufacturer's recommendations when servicing the breaker points.*	3.4
3.4—Connect a dwell meter between the distributor primary lead and ground. Crank the engine and observe the point dwell angle.	If necessary, adjust the point dwell angle: NOTE: *Increasing the point gap decreases the dwell angle, and vice-versa.*	3.6
	If dwell meter shows little or no reading:	3.5

Dwell meter hook-up

Dwell angle

3.5—Check the condenser for short: Connect an ohmmeter across the condenser body and the pigtail lead.	If any reading other than infinite resistance is noted, replace the condenser:	3.6

Checking the condenser for short

Test and Procedure	Results and Indications	Proceed to
3.6—Test the coil primary resistance: Connect an ohmmeter across the coil primary terminals, and read the resistance on the low scale. Note whether an external ballast resistor or resistance wire is utilized.	Coils utilizing ballast resistors or resistance wires should have approximately 1.0Ω resistance; coils with internal resistors should have approximately 4.0Ω resistance. If values far from the above are noted, replace the coil:	4.1

Testing the coil primary resistance

4.1—Check for spark: Hold each spark plug wire approximately $\frac{1}{4}''$ from ground with gloves or a heavy, dry rag. Crank the engine, and observe the spark.	If no spark is evident:	4.2
	If spark is good in some cylinders:	4.3
	If spark is good in all cylinders:	4.6
4.2—Check for spark at the coil high tension lead: Remove the coil high tension lead from the distributor and position it approximately $\frac{1}{4}''$ from ground. Crank the engine and observe spark. CAUTION: *This test should not be performed on cars equipped with transistorized ignition.*	If the spark is good and consistent:	4.3
	If the spark is good but intermittent, test the primary electrical system starting at 3.3:	3.3
	If the spark is weak or non-existent, replace the coil high tension lead, clean and tighten all connections and retest. If no improvement is noted:	4.4
4.3—Visually inspect the distributor cap and rotor for burned or corroded contacts, cracks, carbon tracks, or moisture. Also check the fit of the rotor on the distributor shaft (where applicable).	If moisture is present, dry thoroughly, and retest per 4.1:	4.1
	If burned or excessively corroded contacts, cracks, or carbon tracks are noted, replace the defective part(s) and retest per 4.1:	4.1
	If the rotor and cap appear intact, or are only slightly corroded, clean the contacts thoroughly (including the cap towers and spark plug wire ends) and retest per 4.1: If the spark is good in all cases: If the spark is poor in all cases:	4.6 4.5
4.4—Check the coil secondary resistance: Connect an ohmmeter across the distributor side of the coil and the coil tower. Read the resistance on the high scale of the ohmmeter.	The resistance of a satisfactory coil should be between $4K\Omega$ and $10K\Omega$. If the resistance is considerably higher (i.e., $40K\Omega$) replace the coil, and retest per 4.1: NOTE: *This does not apply to high performance coils.*	4.1

Testing the coil secondary resistance

Test and Procedure	Results and Indications	Proceed to
4.5—Visually inspect the spark plug wires for cracking or brittleness. Ensure that no two wires are positioned so as to cause induction firing (adjacent and parallel). Remove each wire, one by one, and check resistance with an ohmmeter.	Replace any cracked or brittle wires. If any of the wires are defective, replace the entire set. Replace any wires with excessive resistance (over 8000Ω per foot for suppression wire), and separate any wires that might cause induction firing.	4.6
4.6—Remove the spark plugs, noting the cylinders from which they were removed, and evaluate according to the chart below.	See below.	See below.

	Condition	Cause	Remedy	Proceed to
	Electrodes eroded, light brown deposits.	Normal wear. Normal wear is indicated by approximately .001″ wear per 1000 miles.	Clean and regap the spark plug if wear is not excessive: Replace the spark plug if excessively worn:	4.7

	Carbon fouling (black, dry, fluffy deposits).	If present on one or two plugs:
		    Faulty high tension lead(s).
		    Burnt or sticking valve(s).
			Test the high tension leads:
			Check the valve train: (Clean and regap the plugs in either case.)
				4.5
				
				9.1

		If present on most or all plugs: Overly rich fuel mixture, due to restricted air filter, improper carburetor adjustment, improper choke or heat riser adjustment or operation.	Check the fuel system:	5.1
	Oil fouling (wet black deposits)	Worn engine components. NOTE: *Oil fouling may occur in new or recently rebuilt engines until broken in.*	Check engine vacuum and compression: Replace with new spark plug	6.1
	Lead fouling (gray, black, tan, or yellow deposits, which appear glazed or cinderlike).	Combustion by-products.	Clean and regap the plugs: (Use plugs of a different heat range if the problem recurs.)	4.7

	Condition	Cause	Remedy	Proceed to
	Gap bridging (deposits lodged between the electrodes).	Incomplete combustion, or transfer of deposits from the combustion chamber.	Replace the spark plugs:	4.7
	Overheating (burnt electrodes, and extremely white insulator with small black spots).	Ignition timing advanced too far.	Adjust timing to specifications:	8.2
		Overly lean fuel mixture.	Check the fuel system:	5.1
		Spark plugs not seated properly.	Clean spark plug seat and install a new gasket washer: (Replace the spark plugs in all cases.)	4.7
	Fused spot deposits on the insulator.	Combustion chamber blow-by.	Clean and regap the spark plugs:	4.7
	Pre-ignition (melted or severely burned electrodes, blistered or cracked insulators, or metallic deposits on the insulator).	Incorrect spark plug heat range.	Replace with plugs of the proper heat range:	4.7
		Ignition timing advanced too far.	Adjust timing to specifications:	8.2
		Spark plugs not being cooled efficiently.	Clean the spark plug seat, and check the cooling system:	11.1
		Fuel mixture too lean.	Check the fuel system:	5.1
		Poor compression.	Check compression:	6.1
		Fuel grade too low.	Use higher octane fuel:	4.7

Test and Procedure	Results and Indications	Proceed to
4.7—Determine the static ignition timing: Using the flywheel or crankshaft pulley timing marks as a guide, locate top dead center on the *compression* stroke of the No. 1 cylinder. Remove the distributor cap.	Adjust the distributor so that the rotor points toward the No. 1 tower in the distributor cap, and the points are just opening:	4.8
4.8—Check coil polarity: Connect a voltmeter negative lead to the coil high tension lead, and the positive lead to ground (NOTE: *reverse the hook-up for positive ground cars*). Crank the engine momentarily. **Checking coil polarity**	If the voltmeter reads up-scale, the polarity is correct:	5.1
	If the voltmeter reads down-scale, reverse the coil polarity (switch the primary leads):	5.1

Test and Procedure	*Results and Indications*	*Proceed to*
5.1—Determine that the air filter is functioning efficiently: Hold paper elements up to a strong light, and attempt to see light through the filter.	Clean permanent air filters in gasoline (or manufacturer's recommendation), and allow to dry. Replace paper elements through which light cannot be seen:	5.2
5.2—Determine whether a flooding condition exists: Flooding is identified by a strong gasoline odor, and excessive gasoline present in the throttle bore(s) of the carburetor.	If flooding is not evident:	5.3
	If flooding is evident, permit the gasoline to dry for a few moments and restart.	
	If flooding doesn't recur:	5.6
	If flooding is persistant:	5.5
5.3—Check that fuel is reaching the carburetor: Detach the fuel line at the carburetor inlet. Hold the end of the line in a cup (not styrofoam), and crank the engine.	If fuel flows smoothly:	5.6
	If fuel doesn't flow (NOTE: *Make sure that there is fuel in the tank*), or flows erratically:	5.4
5.4—Test the fuel pump: Disconnect all fuel lines from the fuel pump. Hold a finger over the input fitting, crank the engine (with electric pump, turn the ignition or pump on); and feel for suction.	If suction is evident, blow out the fuel line to the tank with low pressure compressed air until bubbling is heard from the fuel filler neck. Also blow out the carburetor fuel line (both ends disconnected):	5.6
	If no suction is evident, replace or repair the fuel pump:	5.6
	NOTE: *Repeated oil fouling of the spark plugs, or a no-start condition, could be the result of a ruptured vacuum booster pump diaphragm, through which oil or gasoline is being drawn into the intake manifold (where applicable).*	
5.5—Check the needle and seat: Tap the carburetor in the area of the needle and seat.	If flooding stops, a gasoline additive (e.g., Gumout) will often cure the problem:	5.6
	If flooding continues, check the fuel pump for excessive pressure at the carburetor (according to specifications). If the pressure is normal, the needle and seat must be removed and checked, and/or the float level adjusted:	5.6
5.6—Test the accelerator pump by looking into the throttle bores while operating the throttle.	If the accelerator pump appears to be operating normally:	5.7
	If the accelerator pump is not operating, the pump must be reconditioned. Where possible, service the pump with the carburetor(s) installed on the engine. If necessary, remove the carburetor. Prior to removal:	5.7
5.7—Determine whether the carburetor main fuel system is functioning: Spray a commercial starting fluid into the carburetor while attempting to start the engine.	If the engine starts, runs for a few seconds, and dies:	5.8
	If the engine doesn't start:	6.1

Test and Procedures	Results and Indications	Proceed to
5.8—Uncommon fuel system malfunctions: See below:	If the problem is solved:	6.1
	If the problem remains, remove and recondition the carburetor.	

Condition	Indication	Test	Usual Weather Conditions	Remedy
Vapor lock	Car will not re-start shortly after running.	Cool the components of the fuel system until the engine starts.	Hot to very hot	Ensure that the exhaust manifold heat control valve is operating. Check with the vehicle manufacturer for the recommended solution to vapor lock on the model in question.
Carburetor icing	Car will not idle, stalls at low speeds.	Visually inspect the throttle plate area of the throttle bores for frost.	High humidity, 32-40° F.	Ensure that the exhaust manifold heat control valve is operating, and that the intake manifold heat riser is not blocked.
Water in the fuel	Engine sputters and stalls; may not start.	Pump a small amount of fuel into a glass jar. Allow to stand, and inspect for droplets or a layer of water.	High humidity, extreme temperature changes.	For droplets, use one or two cans of commercial gas dryer (Dry Gas) For a layer of water, the tank must be drained, and the fuel lines blown out with compressed air.

Test and Procedure	Results and Indications	Proceed to
6.1—Test engine compression: Remove all spark plugs. Insert a compression gauge into a spark plug port, crank the engine to obtain the maximum reading, and record.	If compression is within limits on all cylinders:	7.1
	If gauge reading is extremely low on all cylinders:	6.2
	If gauge reading is low on one or two cylinders:	6.2
	(If gauge readings are identical and low on two or more adjacent cylinders, the head gasket must be replaced.)	

Testing compression
(© Chevrolet Div. G.M. Corp.)

Compression pressure limits
(© Buick Div. G.M. Corp.)

Maxi. Press. Lbs. Sq. In.	Min. Press. Lbs. Sq. In.	Maxi. Press. Lbs. Sq. In.	Min. Press. Lbs. Sq. In.	Max. Press. Lbs. Sq. In.	Min. Press. Lbs. Sq. In.	Max. Press. Lbs. Sq. In.	Min. Press. Lbs. Sq. In.
134	101	162	121	188	141	214	160
136	102	164	123	190	142	216	162
138	104	166	124	192	144	218	163
140	105	168	126	194	145	220	165
142	107	170	127	196	147	222	166
146	110	172	129	198	148	224	168
148	111	174	131	200	150	226	169
150	113	176	132	202	151	228	171
152	114	178	133	204	153	230	172
154	115	180	135	206	154	232	174
156	117	182	136	208	156	234	175
158	118	184	138	210	157	236	177
160	120	186	140	212	158	238	178

Test and Procedure	Results and Indications	Proceed to
6.2—Test engine compression (wet): Squirt approximately 30 cc. of engine oil into each cylinder, and retest per 6.1.	If the readings improve, worn or cracked rings or broken pistons are indicated:	Next Chapter
	If the readings do not improve, burned or excessively carboned valves or a jumped timing chain are indicated:	7.1
	NOTE: *A jumped timing chain is often indicated by difficult cranking.*	
7.1—Perform a vacuum check of the engine: Attach a vacuum gauge to the intake manifold beyond the throttle plate. Start the engine, and observe the action of the needle over the range of engine speeds.	See below.	See below

	Reading	Indications	Proceed to
	Steady, from 17-22 in. Hg.	Normal.	8.1
	Low and steady.	Late ignition or valve timing, or low compression:	6.1
	Very low	Vacuum leak:	7.2
	Needle fluctuates as engine speed increases.	Ignition miss, blown cylinder head gasket, leaking valve or weak valve spring:	6.1, 8.3
	Gradual drop in reading at idle.	Excessive back pressure in the exhaust system:	10.1
	Intermittent fluctuation at idle.	Ignition miss, sticking valve:	8.3, 9.1
	Drifting needle.	Improper idle mixture adjustment, carburetors not synchronized (where applicable), or minor intake leak. Synchronize the carburetors, adjust the idle, and retest. If the condition persists:	7.2
	High and steady.	Early ignition timing:	8.2

Test and Procedure	Results and Indications	Proceed to
7.2—Attach a vacuum gauge per 7.1, and test for an intake manifold leak. Squirt a small amount of oil around the intake manifold gaskets, carburetor gaskets, plugs and fittings. Observe the action of the vacuum gauge.	If the reading improves, replace the indicated gasket, or seal the indicated fitting or plug:	8.1
	If the reading remains low:	7.3
7.3—Test all vacuum hoses and accessories for leaks as described in 7.2. Also check the carburetor body (dashpots, automatic choke mechanism, throttle shafts) for leaks in the same manner.	If the reading improves, service or replace the offending part(s):	8.1
	If the reading remains low:	6.1
8.1—Check the point dwell angle: Connect a dwell meter between the distributor primary wire and ground. Start the engine, and observe the dwell angle from idle to 3000 rpm.	If necessary, adjust the dwell angle. NOTE: *Increasing the point gap reduces the dwell angle and vice-versa.* If the dwell angle moves outside specifications as engine speed increases, the distributor should be removed and checked for cam accuracy, shaft end-play and concentricity, bushing wear, and adequate point arm tension (NOTE: *Most of these items may be checked with the distributor installed in the engine, using an oscilloscope*):	8.2
8.2—Connect a timing light (per manufacturer's recommendation) and check the dynamic ignition timing. Disconnect and plug the vacuum hose(s) to the distributor if specified, start the engine, and observe the timing marks at the specified engine speed.	If the timing is not correct, adjust to specifications by rotating the distributor in the engine: (Advance timing by rotating distributor opposite normal direction of rotor rotation, retard timing by rotating distributor in same direction as rotor rotation.)	8.3
8.3—Check the operation of the distributor advance mechanism(s): To test the mechanical advance, disconnect all but the mechanical advance, and observe the timing marks with a timing light as the engine speed is increased from idle. If the mark moves smoothly, without hesitation, it may be assumed that the mechanical advance is functioning properly. To test vacuum advance and/or retard systems, alternately crimp and release the vacuum line, and observe the timing mark for movement. If movement is noted, the system is operating.	If the systems are functioning:	8.4
	If the systems are not functioning, remove the distributor, and test on a distributor tester:	8.4
8.4—Locate an ignition miss: With the engine running, remove each spark plug wire, one by one, until one is found that doesn't cause the engine to roughen and slow down.	When the missing cylinder is identified:	4.1

Test and Procedure	*Results and Indications*	*Proceed to*
9.1—Evaluate the valve train: Remove the valve cover, and ensure that the valves are adjusted to specifications. A mechanic's stethoscope may be used to aid in the diagnosis of the valve train. By pushing the probe on or near push rods or rockers, valve noise often can be isolated. A timing light also may be used to diagnose valve problems. Connect the light according to manufacturer's recommendations, and start the engine. Vary the firing moment of the light by increasing the engine speed (and therefore the ignition advance), and moving the trigger from cylinder to cylinder. Observe the movement of each valve.	See below	See below

Observation	*Probable Cause*	*Remedy*	*Proceed to*
Metallic tap heard through the stethoscope.	Sticking hydraulic lifter or excessive valve clearance.	Adjust valve. If tap persists, remove and replace the lifter:	10.1
Metallic tap through the stethoscope, able to push the rocker arm (lifter side) down by hand.	Collapsed valve lifter.	Remove and replace the lifter:	10.1
Erratic, irregular motion of the valve stem.*	Sticking valve, burned valve.	Recondition the valve and/or valve guide:	Next Chapter
Eccentric motion of the pushrod at the rocker arm.*	Bent pushrod.	Replace the pushrod:	10.1
Valve retainer bounces as the valve closes.*	Weak valve spring or damper.	Remove and test the spring and damper. Replace if necessary:	10.1

*—When observed with a timing light.

Test and Procedure	*Results and Indications*	*Proceed to*
9.2—Check the valve timing: Locate top dead center of the No. 1 piston, and install a degree wheel or tape on the crankshaft pulley or damper with zero corresponding to an index mark on the engine. Rotate the crankshaft in its direction of rotation, and observe the opening of the No. 1 cylinder intake valve. The opening should correspond with the correct mark on the degree wheel according to specifications.	If the timing is not correct, the timing cover must be removed for further investigation:	

Test and Procedure	Results and Indications	Proceed to
10.1—Determine whether the exhaust manifold heat control valve is operating: Operate the valve by hand to determine whether it is free to move. If the valve is free, run the engine to operating temperature and observe the action of the valve, to ensure that it is opening.	If the valve sticks, spray it with a suitable solvent, open and close the valve to free it, and retest.	
	If the valve functions properly:	10.2
	If the valve does not free, or does not operate, replace the valve:	10.2
10.2—Ensure that there are no exhaust restrictions: Visually inspect the exhaust system for kinks, dents, or crushing. Also note that gasses are flowing freely from the tailpipe at all engine speeds, indicating no restriction in the muffler or resonator.	Replace any damaged portion of the system:	11.1
11.1—Visually inspect the fan belt for glazing, cracks, and fraying, and replace if necessary. Tighten the belt so that the longest span has approximately ½″ play at its midpoint under thumb pressure.	Replace or tighten the fan belt as necessary:	11.2

Checking the fan belt tension
(© Nissan Motor Co. Ltd.)

Test and Procedure	Results and Indications	Proceed to
11.2—Check the fluid level of the cooling system.	If full or slightly low, fill as necessary:	11.5
	If extremely low:	11.3
11.3—Visually inspect the external portions of the cooling system (radiator, radiator hoses, thermostat elbow, water pump seals, heater hoses, etc.) for leaks. If none are found, pressurize the cooling system to 14-15 psi.	If cooling system holds the pressure:	11.5
	If cooling system loses pressure rapidly, re-inspect external parts of the system for leaks under pressure. If none are found, check dipstick for coolant in crankcase. If no coolant is present, but pressure loss continues:	11.4
	If coolant is evident in crankcase, remove cylinder head(s), and check gasket(s). If gaskets are intact, block and cylinder head(s) should be checked for cracks or holes.	
	If the gasket(s) is blown, replace, and purge the crankcase of coolant:	12.6
	NOTE: *Occasionally, due to atmospheric and driving conditions, condensation of water can occur in the crankcase. This causes the oil to appear milky white. To remedy, run the engine until hot, and change the oil and oil filter.*	

Test and Procedure	Results and Indication	Proceed to
11.4—Check for combustion leaks into the cooling system: Pressurize the cooling system as above. Start the engine, and observe the pressure gauge. If the needle fluctuates, remove each spark plug wire, one by one, noting which cylinder(s) reduce or eliminate the fluctuation. **Radiator pressure tester** (© American Motors Corp.)	Cylinders which reduce or eliminate the fluctuation, when the spark plug wire is removed, are leaking into the cooling system. Replace the head gasket on the affected cylinder bank(s).	
11.5—Check the radiator pressure cap: Attach a radiator pressure tester to the radiator cap (wet the seal prior to installation). Quickly pump up the pressure, noting the point at which the cap releases. **Testing the radiator pressure cap** (© American Motors Corp.)	If the cap releases within ± 1 psi of the specified rating, it is operating properly: If the cap releases at more than ± 1 psi of the specified rating, it should be replaced:	11.6 11.6
11.6—Test the thermostat: Start the engine cold, remove the radiator cap, and insert a thermometer into the radiator. Allow the engine to idle. After a short while, there will be a sudden, rapid increase in coolant temperature. The temperature at which this sharp rise stops is the thermostat opening temperature.	If the thermostat opens at or about the specified temperature: If the temperature doesn't increase: (If the temperature increases slowly and gradually, replace the thermostat.)	11.7 11.7
11.7—Check the water pump: Remove the thermostat elbow and the thermostat, disconnect the coil high tension lead (to prevent starting), and crank the engine momentarily.	If coolant flows, replace the thermostat and retest per 11.6: If coolant doesn't flow, reverse flush the cooling system to alleviate any blockage that might exist. If system is not blocked, and coolant will not flow, recondition the water pump.	11.6 —
12.1—Check the oil pressure gauge or warning light: If the gauge shows low pressure, or the light is on, for no obvious reason, remove the oil pressure sender. Install an accurate oil pressure gauge and run the engine momentarily.	If oil pressure builds normally, run engine for a few moments to determine that it is functioning normally, and replace the sender. If the pressure remains low: If the pressure surges: If the oil pressure is zero:	— 12.2 12.3 12.3

Test and Procedure	*Results and Indications*	*Proceed to*
12.2—Visually inspect the oil: If the oil is watery or very thin, milky, or foamy, replace the oil and oil filter.	If the oil is normal:	12.3
	If after replacing oil the pressure remains low:	12.3
	If after replacing oil the pressure becomes normal:	—
12.3—Inspect the oil pressure relief valve and spring, to ensure that it is not sticking or stuck. Remove and thoroughly clean the valve, spring, and the valve body. **Oil pressure relief valve** (© British Leyland Motors)	If the oil pressure improves:	—
	If no improvement is noted:	12.4
12.4—Check to ensure that the oil pump is not cavitating (sucking air instead of oil): See that the crankcase is neither over nor underfull, and that the pickup in the sump is in the proper position and free from sludge.	Fill or drain the crankcase to the proper capacity, and clean the pickup screen in solvent if necessary. If no improvement is noted:	12.5
12.5—Inspect the oil pump drive and the oil pump:	If the pump drive or the oil pump appear to be defective, service as necessary and retest per 12.1:	12.1
	If the pump drive and pump appear to be operating normally, the engine should be disassembled to determine where blockage exists:	Next Chapter
12.6—Purge the engine of ethylene glycol coolant: Completely drain the crankcase and the oil filter. Obtain a commercial butyl cellosolve base solvent, designated for this purpose, and follow the instructions precisely. Following this, install a new oil filter and refill the crankcase with the proper weight oil. The next oil and filter change should follow shortly thereafter (1000 miles).		

3 · Engine and Engine Rebuilding

Engine Electrical

DISTRIBUTOR

Removal

1. Remove the high-tension wires from the distributor cap terminal towers, noting their positions to assure correct reassembly.

2. Remove the primary lead from the coil terminal.

3. Disconnect the vacuum line.

4. Unlatch the two distributor cap retaining clips and remove the distributor cap.

5. Note the position of the rotor in relation to the base. Scribe a mark on the base of the distributor and on the engine block to facilitate reinstallation. Align the marks with the direction the metal tip of the rotor is pointing.

6. Remove the bolt which holds the distributor to the engine.

7. Lift the distributor assembly from the engine.

Installation

1. Insert the distributor shaft and assembly into the engine. Line up the mark on the distributor and the one on the engine with the metal tip of the rotor. Make sure that the vacuum advance diaphragm is pointed in the same direction as it was pointed originally. This will be done automatically if the marks on the engine and the distributor are lined up with the rotor.

2. Install the distributor hold-down bolt and clamp. Leave the screw loose enough so that you can move the distributor with heavy hand pressure.

3. Connect the primary wire to the coil. Install the distributor cap on the distributor housing. Secure the distributor cap with the spring clips.

4. Install the spark plug wires. Make sure that the wires are pressed all the way into the top of the distributor cap and firmly onto the spark plug.

5. Adjust the point dwell and set the ignition timing.

NOTE: *If the crankshaft has been turned or the engine disturbed in any manner (i.e., disassembled and rebuilt) while the distributor was removed, or if the marks were not drawn, it will be necessary to initially time the engine. Follow the procedure given below.*

1. It is necessary to place the No. 1 cylinder in the firing position to correctly install the distributor. To locate this position, the ignition timing marks on the crankshaft front pulley are used.

2. Remove the No. 1 cylinder spark plug. Turn the crankshaft until the piston in the No. 1 cylinder is moving up on the compression stroke. This can be

determined by placing your thumb over the spark plug hole and feeling the air being forced out of the cylinder. Stop turning the crankshaft when the timing marks that are used to time the engine are aligned.

3. Oil the distributor housing lightly where the distributor bears on the cylinder block.

4. Install the distributor so that the rotor, which is mounted on the shaft, points toward the No. 1 spark plug terminal tower position when the cap is installed. Of course you won't be able to see the direction in which the rotor is pointing if the cap is on the distributor. Lay the cap on the top of the distributor and make a mark on the side of the distributor housing just below the No. 1 spark plug terminal. Make sure that the rotor points toward that mark when you install the distributor.

5. When the distributor shaft has reached the bottom of the hole, move the rotor back and forth slightly until the driving lug on the end of the shaft enters the slots cut in the end of the oil pump shaft and the distributor assembly slides down into place.

6. When the distributor is correctly installed, the breaker points should be in such a position that they are just ready to break contact with each other. This is accomplished by rotating the distributor body after it has been installed in the engine. Once again, line up the marks that you made before the distributor was removed from the engine.

7. Install the distributor hold-down bolt.

8. Install the spark plug into the No. 1 spark plug hole and continue from Step 3 of the distributor installation procedure.

Firing Order

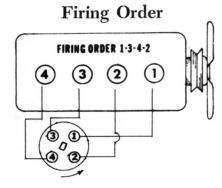

FIRING ORDER 1-3-4-2

ALTERNATOR

All Chevrolet LUV vehicles are equipped with a 30 amp alternator with an electromechanical, adjustable voltage regulator.

Alternator Precautions

To prevent damage to the alternator and regulator, the following precautionary measures must be taken when working with the electrical system.

1. Never reverse battery connections. Always check the battery polarity visually. This is to be done before any connections are made to be sure that all of the connections correspond to the battery ground polarity of the LUV.

2. Booster batteries for starting must be connected properly. Make sure that the positive cable of the booster battery is connected to the positive terminal of the battery that is getting the boost. This applies to both negative and ground cables.

3. Disconnect the battery cables before using a fast charger; the charger has a tendency to force current through the diodes in the opposite direction for which they were designed. This burns out the diodes.

4. Never use a fast charger as a booster for starting the vehicle.

5. Never disconnect the voltage regulator while the engine is running.

6. Do not ground the alternator output terminal.

7. Do not operate the alternator on an open circuit with the field energized.

8. Do not attempt to polarize an alternator.

Removal and Installation

1. Remove the air pump.

2. Disconnect the battery ground cable before disconnecting the cable from the alternator "A" terminal. This is a hot cable connected directly to the battery.

3. Disconnect the alternator circuit at the connector and disconnect the cable from the "A" terminal.

4. Remove the mounting bolts on the lower part of the alternator and the fan belt adjusting bolt and remove the alternator.

5. Install the alternator in the reverse order of removal and tighten the fan belt and air pump belt tension.

Alternator and Regulator Specifications

	ALTERNATOR			REGULATOR					
					Field Relay		Regulator		
Year	Part No.	Field Current @ 12V (amps)	Output (amps)	Part No.	Core Gap (in.)	Point Gap (in.)	Core Gap (in.)	Point Gap (in.)	Volts @ 75° F
All	LT 130–83	1.2–1.7	30	TL1Z66	.032–.039	.016–.024	.024–.039	.012–.016	13.5–14.5

REGULATOR

Removal and Installation

1. Remove the negative battery cable from the battery.
2. Disconnect the electrical leads at the regulator, taking note to the positions in order to facilitate correct reconnection.
3. Remove the two mounting screws and remove the regulator.
4. Install the regulator in the reverse order of removal.

Adjustment

1. Remove the regulator from the vehicle and remove the regulator cover.
2. If the contact points are rough, dress them with fine sandpaper.
3. Check and adjust the gaps: core gap first, and then the point gap. Adjustment of the yoke gap is unnecessary.
4. Adjust the core gap by loosening the screws attaching the contact set to the yoke. Move the contact set up or down as required. The standard core gap is 0.024-0.039 in. Tighten the attaching screw.
5. Adjust the point gap by loosening the screw attaching the upper contact.

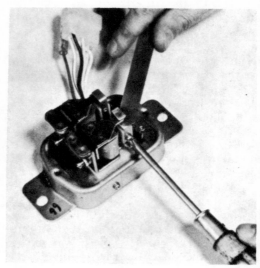

Adjusting the regulator point gap

Move the upper contact up or down as required. The standard point gap is 0.012-0.016 in.
6. Adjust the regulated voltage by means of the adjusting screw. Turn the adjusting screw in to increase voltage and out to reduce voltage. When the correct adjustment is obtained, secure the adjusting screw by tightening the locknut. The regulated voltage is 13.5-14.5 volts.
7. Install the regulator cover, reconnect the electrical leads and install the regulator.

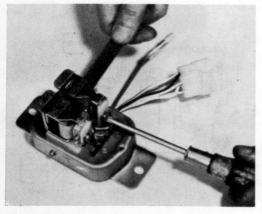

Adjusting the regulator core gap

Adjusting the regulator voltage

Battery and Starter Specifications

| | Battery | | | Starter | | | | | | |
| | | | | Lock Test | | | No Load Test | | | |
Year	Amp Hour Capacity	Volts	Ground	Amps	Volts	Torque (ft lbs)	Amps	Volts	RPM	Brush Spring Tension (lbs)
All	50	12	Neg	330 or less	5.1	5.8	60 or less	12	6000+	1.76

STARTER

Removal and Installation

1. Disconnect the negative battery cable from the battery.

2. Disconnect the starter wiring at the starter, taking note of the positions for correct reinstallation.

3. Remove the bolts attaching the starter to the engine and remove the starter from the vehicle.

4. Install the starter in the reverse order of removal.

Brush Replacement

1. With the starter out of the vehicle, remove the bolts holding the solenoid to the top of the starter and remove the solenoid.

2. To remove the brushes, remove the two thru-bolts and the two rear cover attaching screws and remove the rear cover.

3. Disconnect the brushes electrical leads and remove the brushes.

4. Install the brushes in the reverse order of removal.

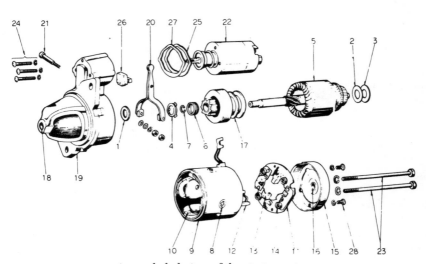

An exploded view of the starter motor

1. Thrust washer
2. Spacer
3. Washer
4. Stopper washer
5. Armature
6. Pinion stopper
7. Snap-ring
8. Field coil retaining screw
9. Yoke housing
10. Field coils
11. Brush holder
12. Brush (field coil)
13. Brush (ground)
14. Brush tension spring
15. Rear cover
16. Rear armature bearing
17. Clutch drive
18. Front armature bearing
19. Gear case
20. Shift lever
21. Shift lever pivot bolt
22. Solenoid switch
23. Through-bolts
24. Solenoid-to-gear case attaching bolts
25. Washer
26. Dust cover
27. Insulator
28. Brush holder-to-rear cover attaching screw

Starter Drive Replacement

1. With the starter motor removed from the vehicle, remove the solenoid from the starter.

2. Remove the two thru-bolts and separate the gear case from the yoke housing.

3. Remove the pinion stopper clip and the pinion stopper.

4. Slide the starter drive off the armature shaft.

5. Install the starter drive and reassemble the starter in the reverse order of removal.

Engine Mechanical

DESIGN

The engine used in the LUV is a water-cooled, 4 cycle, 4 cylinder, overhead camshaft gasoline engine.

The cylinder head is cast aluminum alloy with wedge-type combustion chambers.

The valve system consists of a chain-driven overhead camshaft and unequally pitched valve springs.

The crankshaft is supported by five main bearings.

ENGINE REMOVAL AND INSTALLATION

1. Disconnect the battery ground cable.

2. Prior to removing the hood, scribe a mark in the area of the hinges to ensure that the hood is reinstalled in its original position. Remove the hood.

3. Drain the cooling system through the drain cock on the radiator and on the cylinder block.

4. Drain the engine oil.

5. Disconnect the upper and lower hoses from the radiator and remove the radiator.

6. Disconnect the hoses from the air cleaner and remove the air cleaner assembly.

7. Remove the carburetor control cable.

8. Remove the choke control cable.

9. Disconnect the carburetor wiring.

10. Disconnect the exhaust pipe from the exhaust manifold at the flange.

11. Disconnect the generator and starter wiring.

12. Disconnect the heater hose at the fender side.

13. Disconnect the vacuum hose.

14. Disconnect the spark plug wires from the distributor.

15. Disconnect the grounding cable between the cylinder head cover and the dashboard at the cylinder head cover side.

16. Disconnect the engine wiring at the two connectors.

17. Disconnect the oil pressure unit cord and temperature sending unit lead and the distributor ground wire; remove the wire from the three clips on the engine.

18. Disconnect the fuel line from the fuel pump.

19. Disconnect the ground cable on the timing gear case at the engine side.

20. Disconnect the two hoses from the fuel tank evaporative emission control check and relief valve.

21. Disconnect the driveshaft at the rear axle.

22. Remove the driveshaft from the transmission and install a plug in the end of the transmission to prevent loss of lubricant.

23. Disconnect the clutch slave cylinder.

24. Remove the exhaust pipe bracket from the clutch housing.

25. Disconnect the speedometer drive cable at the transmission.

26. Disconnect the body grounding cable between the transmission and the body at the floor side.

27. Remove the gearshift lever assembly.

28. Insert a lifting device into the engine hangers and lift the engine slightly.

29. Remove the engine rear mounts.

30. Check that the engine and auxiliary parts are separated completely from the chassis frame then, lift the engine out of position. When hoisting the engine, adjust the tension so that the front end of the engine is elevated slightly above the rear of the engine.

31. When the front of the engine clears the deflector, continue raising and

General Engine Specifications

Year	Engine Displacement cu in. (cc)	Carb Type	Advertised Horsepower (@ rpm)	Advertised Torque @ rpm (ft lbs)	Bore and Stroke (in.)	Advertised Compression Ratio	Oil Pressure (psi)
1972–74	110.8 (1817)	2661	75 @ 5000	88 @ 3000	3.31 x 3.23	8.2 : 1	57

Valve Specifications

Year	Engine Displacement cu in. (cc)	Seat Angle (deg)	Face Angle (deg)	Spring Test Pressure (lbs @ in.) Outer	Inner	Free Length (in.) Outer	Inner	Stem-to-Guide Clearance (in.) Intake	Exhaust	Stem Diameter (in.) Intake	Exhaust
1972–74	110.8 (1817)	45	45	41.8–50.1 @ 1.58	15.4–19.0 @ 1.50	2.05–1.99	1.78–1.73	.0016–.0079	.0020–.0098	.3150–.3102	.3150–.3091

Crankshaft and Connecting Rod Specifications
(All measurements given in in.)

Year	Engine Displacement cu in. (cc)	Crankshaft Main Brg Journal Dia	Main Brg Oil Clearance	Shaft End-Play	Thrust on No.	Connecting Rod Journal Dia	Oil Clearance	Side Clearance
1972–74	110.8 (1817)	2.2016–2.2022	0.0016–0.0047	0.0059–0.0120	3	1.9262–1.9268	0.0020–0.0047	0.0079–0.0130

Ring Side Clearance

Year	Engine Displacement cu in. (cc)	Top Compression (in.) Min	Max	Replace	Bottom Compression (in.) Min	Max	Replace	Oil Control (in.) Min	Max
All	110.8 (1817)	0.0012	0.0028	0.0120	0.0012	0.0028	0.0120	0.0008	0.0024①

① Replace when 0.0060 in.

Torque Specifications
(All readings in ft lbs unless noted)

Year	Engine Displacement cu in. (cc)	Cylinder Head Bolts	Rod Bearing Bolts	Main Bearing Bolts	Crankshaft Pulley Bolt	Flywheel-to-Crankshaft	Manifolds Intake	Exhaust
All	110.8 (1817)	①	43	72	50	36②	N.A.	N.A.

① On 1972 models, tighten to 43 ft lbs first, then completely loosen and retighten to 58 ft lbs. On 1973 models, tighten, in sequence, to 60 ft lbs. On 1974–75 models, tighten to 43 ft lbs first, then loosen completely and retighten 1, 2, 3, and 6 to 70 ft lbs, and the remaining bolts to 60 ft lbs.
② 69 ft lbs in 1974
N.A. Not available

Ring Gaps

Year	Engine Displacement cu in. (cc)	Top Compression (in.)		Bottom Compression (in.)		Oil Control (in.)	
		Min	Max	Min	Max	Min	Max
All	110.8 (1817)	0.008	0.016①	0.008	0.016①	0.012	0.039

① Replace when 0.059 in.

Piston Clearance

Year	Engine Displacement cu in. (cc)	Minimum (in.)	Maximum (in.)
All	110.8 (1817)	0.0018	0.0026

move the engine toward the front of the truck.

32. Install the engine in the reverse order of removal. After the installation is complete, fill the crankcase with oil, the cooling system with coolant, adjust the clutch pedal free-play, and start the engine and check for leaks.

CYLINDER HEAD

Removal and Installation

1. Disconnect the negative battery cable, drain the cooling system and remove the air cleaner and attending hoses.
2. Remove the air pump.
3. Remove the alternator.
4. Disconnect the carburetor throttle linkage and fuel line together with the solenoid electrical lead.
5. Disconnect the exhaust pipe from the exhaust manifold.
6. Remove the six bolts retaining the camshaft carrier front cover and remove the front cover.
7. Remove the oil line from the secondary chain tensioner plug.
8. Remove the chain tensioner plug along with the tensioner spring.
9. Remove the bolt and plate washer retaining the timing (camshaft) sprocket.
10. Remove both upper secondary

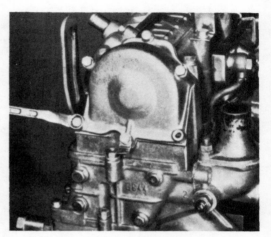

Removing the camshaft carrier front cover

Removing the camshaft timing sprocket retaining bolt

timing chain damper bolts, located in the front of the cylinder head.

11. Loosen both lower timing chain damper bolts.
12. Separate the timing (camshaft) sprocket from the camshaft, together with the chain.

13. Carefully separate the sprocket from the chain to prevent the timing sprocket pin from falling out.

NOTE: *When removing the camshaft from the timing sprocket, the pin should be positioned in the top. Mark the position of the pin on the timing sprocket prior to disassembling the parts.*

14. Hold the chain in position with a wire or cord.

15. Remove the 10 bolts retaining the camshaft cover and remove the cover.

16. Loosen the 12 camshaft carrier bolts evenly in progression and remove them. The camshaft carrier is under tension from the valve springs. Loosen all the bolts alternately in progression, so that a single bolt will not receive the tension of the valve springs. Care must be taken not to loosen the camshaft carrier locating dowel.

Removal of the air injection nozzle

17. Loosen the sleeve nut on the air injection nozzle and remove the nozzle by turning it about 180°.

18. Remove the three bolts retaining the timing gear case to the cylinder head.

19. Loosen the cylinder head bolts in a progressional sequence.

20. Remove the cylinder head, gasket and O-rings.

Install the cylinder head in the reverse order of removal, as follows.

21. Position the cylinder head gasket on the block with the "Top" side up. Insert the O-rings into the oil ports.

22. Position a gear case-to-cylinder head gasket on the gear case, if necessary.

23. Install the cylinder head on the block and tighten the cylinder head bolts to specifications.

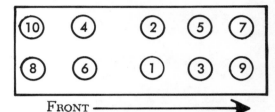

FRONT ————————————————→

Cylinder head bolt tightening sequence

24. Tighten the three bolts attaching the timing gear case to the cylinder head.

25. Install the air injection nozzles. Do not tighten them securely at this time.

26. Align the setting mark on the camshaft thrust plate with the corresponding mark on the camshaft.

27. Position the O-rings to the camshaft carrier. Install these parts in position and lightly tighten the bolts retaining the dowels. Install the longest bolts in the position of the dowel.

28. Install the camshaft carrier bolts. Tighten the bolts alternately, in progression to 15 ft lbs to compress the valve springs evenly. Note that the camshaft carrier is also used to retain two portions of the air manifold bracket and PCV hose clips.

29. With the No. 4 cylinder at TDC of the compression stroke, check that the setting mark on the camshaft and on the thrust plate are correctly aligned. If the setting marks are not in good alignment, make the necessary adjustment as follows:

a. If the setting mark on the camshaft and the thrust plate are not in alignment, attach the camshaft sprocket to the camshaft, insert the pin into a hole in the camshaft timing sprocket and turn the crankshaft until the marks line up. Then, bring the camshaft into a free state by removing the camshaft timing sprocket from the camshaft and, set the piston in the

Camshaft timing marks

No. 4 cylinder to TDC of the compression stroke. If the engine has been turned in reverse in the course of this adjustment, make a final adjustment by turning the engine in the normal direction of rotation so that the marks are lined up, with the chain properly tensioned on the correct side.

b. When installing the camshaft timing sprocket on the camshaft, keep their mating faces free of foreign matter because the drive torque is relayed to the timing sprocket from the camshaft by means of frictional contact.

30. Bring the camshaft timing sprocket together with the timing chain, so that the punched mark on the sprocket is located at the 12 o'clock position. Assemble the sprocket to the camshaft.

31. Adjust the position of the camshaft timing sprocket, relative to the camshaft, so that the punched mark on the camshaft timing sprocket is turned up when the drive side of the timing chain is tensioned by pushing the chain tensioner shoe from the plug hole in the secondary chain tensioner. When the camshaft timing sprocket is correctly installed, the punched mark on the sprocket is brought to a position 6° 20' from the top in the direction of rotation.

32. Hold the parts in their relative position. Look through each of the five holes in the camshaft timing sprocket to find a hole in alignment with the hole in the camshaft flange and insert the pin into that hole.

33. Tighten the camshaft timing sprocket attaching bolt, with the plate washer installed, to 33 ft lbs.

34. Install the camshaft carrier front cover.

35. Install the secondary chain tensioner.

36. Assemble the remaining components to the engine in the reverse order of removal, working backwards from Step 5.

37. Adjust the valves.

Valve Guide Replacement

1. With the cylinder head removed from the vehicle and the valves removed from the head, drive the guides out toward the upper face of the cylinder head with a suitable driver. The valve guides cannot be driven out downward because they are secured in place with a snapring.

2. Lubricate the outside of the new valve guide with oil. Press it all the way into position, from the upper face of the cylinder head, until it is brought in contact with the snap-ring. Allowable interference between the cylinder head and the valve guide is 0.0016 in.

VALVE ROCKERS

Removal and Installation

1. Remove the camshaft carrier as outlined under "Cylinder Head Removal."

2. Remove the rocker spring from the pivot and lift the rocker from the cylinder head. Be careful not to lose the rocker guide resting on the top of each of the valves.

3. Install in the reverse order of removal.

INTAKE AND EXHAUST MANIFOLDS

Removal and Installation

Although the two manifolds are separate pieces, they are removed and installed as a unit.

1. Remove the air cleaner assembly together with all of the attending hoses.

2. Disconnect all of the electrical leads, throttle linkage, fuel and vacuum lines from the carburetor.

3. The carburetor can be removed from the manifold at this point or can be

Removing/installing the rocker retaining spring

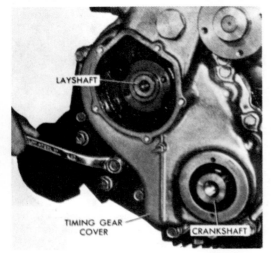

Removing the timing case cover. The layshaft in the illustration is the jackshaft referred to in the text

removed as an assembly with the intake manifold.

4. Disconnect the exhaust pipe from the exhaust manifold.

5. Slightly loosen all of the manifold attaching nuts, and then remove them, working from the outside toward the center. Remove the two manifolds.

6. Install the manifolds in the reverse order of removal, making sure that the mating surfaces are clean before installation.

TIMING GEAR COVER

Removal and Installation

1. Disconnect the negative battery cable from the battery, drain the cooling

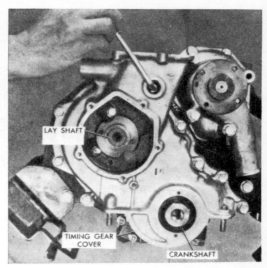

With the access plug removed, remove the bolt on the inner face of the gear cover. The layshaft is the jackshaft referred to in the text

system, and remove the alternator and air pump together with their respective mounting brackets and drive belts.

2. Remove the crankshaft pulley bolt and remove the pulley.

3. Remove the six bolts retaining the front cover and remove the front camshaft carrier cover.

4. Remove the 17 bolts retaining the timing gear case.

5. Remove the access plug and take out the bolt on the inner face of the gear case.

6. Insert the edge of a screwdriver into the cutaway portions on the outer rim of the timing gear case and pry it off the engine.

7. Install the timing gear case and the camshaft carrier front cover in the reverse order of removal and assemble the engine in the reverse order of disassembly.

TIMING CHAINS, SPROCKETS, AND TENSIONERS

Removal and Installation

1. Disconnect the battery ground cable, drain the cooling system, and remove the alternator and air pump together with their respective mounting brackets and drive belts. Remove the cooling fan.

2. Remove the timing gear cover.

3. Remove the oil line from the secondary chain tensioner plug.

4. Remove the chain tensioner plug with the tensioner spring.

5. Remove the bolt and plate washer retaining the camshaft timing sprocket.

6. Remove both of the upper secondary timing chain damper bolts, located in the front of the cylinder head.

7. Loosen both of the lower timing chain damper bolts.

8. Separate the timing sprocket from the camshaft, together with the chain. Then, carefully remove the timing sprocket from the chain to prevent the timing sprocket pin from falling out. When removing the timing sprocket from the camshaft, the pin should be positioned at the top. Mark the position of the pin on the timing sprocket before disassembling the parts.

9. Remove the bolt retaining the secondary timing sprocket to the jackshaft. Remove the secondary sprocket by alternately screwing two bolts into the threaded holes in the timing sprocket one turn at a time.

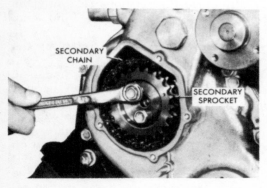

Removing the secondary timing sprocket from the jackshaft by installing two screws in the holes provided and turning them alternately

10. Remove the secondary sprocket from the chain.

11. Remove the chain from the top, through the camshaft carrier front cover hole.

12. Remove the secondary chain tensioners from the cylinder head.

13. Remove the two nuts retaining the primary chain tensioner. Be careful to prevent the tensioner shoe from jumping out of position by the action of the spring. Remove the chain tensioner.

14. Remove the timing sprockets

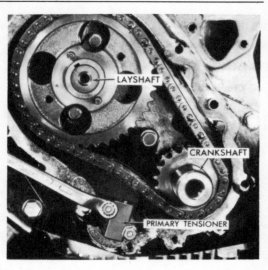

Removing the primary chain tensioner. The layshaft is the jackshaft referred to in the text

together with the chain, by inserting screws into the threaded holes in the jackshaft sprocket and turning them alternately and evenly until the sprockets are free.

To install the timing chains, tensioners and sprockets:

15. If the engine was not disturbed while the components were removed, then install everything in the reverse order of removal, using the procedure below as a guide. If, however, the crankshaft or camshaft was turned or the engine disassembled further, start the assembly procedure by bringing the No. 1 and No. 4 pistons to top dead center (TDC).

16. Check that the pistons are at TDC by positioning the timing gear cover on the locating dowels and place the crankshaft pulley in position. The TDC timing mark should be in direct line with the timing mark pointer.

17. Position the crankshaft and jackshaft timing sprocket into position with the primary chain attached to them. When installing the primary timing sprockets, the timing mark on the jackshaft sprocket must align with the timing mark on the crankshaft sprocket.

18. Align the keyway of the jackshaft with the key in the sprocket by turning the jackshaft, then set both sprockets in position by lightly tapping each sprocket alternately.

NOTE: *The jackshaft can be pre-*

With the No. 1 and 4 pistons at TDC, install the crankshaft and jackshaft sprockets with the chain so that the timing marks on the sprockets are aligned

vented from turning while driving the sprockets into position by holding it through the fuel pump opening.

19. Install the primary chain tensioner.

20. Install a new oil seal in the timing gear case and fill the space between the lips of the oil seal with grease. Position a new gasket to the mating face of the gear case with adhesive. Align the locating dowels with the proper holes and mount the gear case onto the engine. Install and tighten the retaining screws.

21. With the No. 4 piston at TDC on the compression stroke, check to make sure that the setting mark on the camshaft and on the camshaft thrust plate are aligned. If they are not aligned, proceed as follows. If they are aligned, go on to the next numbered step.

   a. Attach the camshaft sprocket to the camshaft, insert the pin into a hole in the camshaft sprocket and turn the crankshaft until the marks on the camshaft and the thrust plate align.

   b. Remove the camshaft sprocket from the camshaft and bring the No. 4 piston to TDC of the compression stroke.

NOTE: *If the engine has been turned in the opposite direction of normal rotation to align the marks on the thrust plate and the camshaft, make the final adjustment by turning the engine in the direction of normal rotation so*

that the marks are lined up and the chain is tensioned on the normal side.

22. Insert the timing chain into the gear case from the upper opening and hold it in position.

23. Bring the jackshaft timing sprocket together with the chain, and install it in position so that the punched mark on the sprocket is pointed to the key on the jackshaft. When the sprocket is correctly installed, the punched mark is located approximately at the 2 o'clock position.

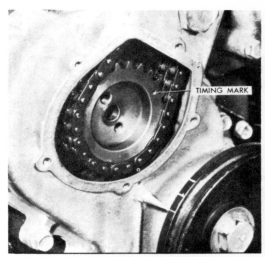

Install the jackshaft secondary timing sprocket so that the punched mark aligns with the key on the jackshaft

24. Bring the camshaft timing sprocket together with the timing chain, so that the punched mark on the sprocket is located at the 12 o'clock position and assemble the sprocket to the camshaft.

25. Adjust the position of the camshaft timing sprocket, relative to the camshaft, so that the punched mark on the camshaft timing sprocket is turned up when the drive side of the timing chain is tensioned by pushing the chain tensioner shoe from the plug hole in the secondary chain tensioner.

NOTE: *When the camshaft timing sprocket is correctly installed, the punched mark on the sprocket is brought to a position 6° 20' from the top in the direction of normal rotation.*

26. Hold all of the parts in position and look through each of the five holes in the camshaft timing sprocket to find a

hole in alignment with the hole in the camshaft flange. Insert the pin into that hole.

27. Tighten the jackshaft timing sprocket attaching bolt to 33 ft lbs. Install the plate washer and tighten the camshaft timing sprocket attaching bolt to 33 ft lbs.

28. Install the gear case front cover and the camshaft carrier front cover.

29. Install the secondary chain tensioner.

30. Assemble the remaining components in the reverse order of removal.

CAMSHAFT

Removal and Installation

1. Remove the camshaft carrier as outlined under the "Cylinder Head Removal and Installation" procedure.

2. Remove the two bolts retaining the thrust plate in position on the front of the camshaft carrier.

3. Remove the thrust plate and carefully slide the camshaft out through the front of the carrier.

Removing the camshaft thrust plate

4. Install the camshaft in the carrier in the reverse order of removal, coating it liberally with engine oil before sliding it into position. Exercise care not to damage the camshaft bearing journals during the installation.

PISTONS AND CONNECTING RODS

Removal and Installation

1. Remove the cylinder head.

2. Remove the oil pan and crankcase.

3. Remove any carbon buildup from the cylinder wall at the top end of the piston travel with a ridge reamer tool.

4. Position the piston to be removed at the bottom of its stroke so that the connecting rod bearing cap can be reached easily from under the engine.

5. Unscrew the connecting rod bearing cap and remove the cap and lower half of the bearing.

6. Push the piston and connecting rod up and out of the cylinder block with a length of wood. Use care not to scratch the cylinder wall with the connecting rod or the wooden tool.

7. Keep all of the components from each cylinder together and install them in the cylinder from which they were removed.

8. Coat the bearing face of the connecting rod and the outer face of the pistons with engine oil.

9. Turn the top compression ring to bring its gap to the side of the piston marked "Front". Set the remaining rings so that their gaps are positioned 120° apart around the piston.

10. Turn the crankshaft until the rod journal of the particular cylinder you are working on is brought to the TDC position.

11. With the piston and rings clamped in a ring compressor, the notched mark on the head of the piston toward the front of the engine, and the marked side of the connecting rod toward the jackshaft, push the piston and connecting rod assembly into the cylinder bore until the big bearing end of the connecting rod contacts and is seated on the rod journal of the crankshaft. Use care not to scratch the cylinder wall with the connecting rod.

12. Push down farther on the piston and turn the crankshaft while the connecting rod rides around on the crankshaft rod journal. Turn the crankshaft until the crankshaft rod journal is at BDC (bottom dead center).

13. Align the mark on the connecting rod bearing cap with that on the con-

necting rod and tighten the bearing cap bolts to the specified torque.

14. Install all of the piston/connecting rod assemblies in the manner outlined above and assemble the oil pan and cylinder head to the engine in the reverse order of removal.

Piston and Connecting Rod Identification and Positioning

The pistons are marked with the word "Front" and a notch in the piston head. When installed in the engine the "Front" and notch markings are to be facing the front of the engine. The connecting rods are numbered corresponding to the cylinders in which they are to be installed. Install the connecting rods in their correct cylinders with the marking to the right of the notch in the piston (looking from the rear of the engine), on the same side as the jackshaft.

Engine Lubrication

OIL PAN

Removal and Installation

In 1972 the LUV engine had an oil pan made up of two different sections: a cast aluminum crankcase attached to the cylinder block and a stamped steel oil pan attached to the crankcase. All other models have a one-piece stamped steel oil pan.

The two-piece crankcase/oil pan used on 1972 models

The tightening sequence for the oil pan used on 1973–74 models

To remove the oil pan it may be necessary to unbolt the motor mounts and jack the engine to gain clearance. Remove the attaching screws and remove the oil pan and/or crankcase. Install in the reverse order of removal, using new gaskets. Tighten the retaining bolts to 50 in. lbs. on models without the separate crankcase; 15 ft lbs on those with a separate crankcase.

REAR MAIN OIL SEAL

Replacement

1972

1. Remove the crankshaft. It is advised that the engine be removed from the vehicle.

2. Remove the old oil seal from the cylinder block and the rear bearing cap.

3. Press the upper half of the seal evenly into position in the cylinder block with a large piece of smooth wooden dowel or similar tool. Trim the ends of the seal so that they are flush with the bearing cap mating surface.

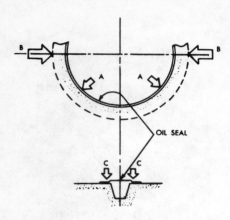

Installation of the rear main oil seal on 1972 models. Press areas "A" into the groove until smooth and even. Trim the excess material from areas "B" and "C".

Also, trim any portion of the seal which overhangs the groove.

4. Install the lower half of the seal in the groove in the rear main bearing cap. Trim the ends of the seal so that they are flush with the mating surface of the cap.

5. Install and assemble in the reverse order of removal.

NOTE: *Install the thrust plates on either side of the No. 3 main bearing journal with the smooth side toward the crankshaft.*

1973–74

1. Remove the oil pan and remove the rear main oil seal retainer from the cylinder block.

2. Fill the space between the lips of the oil seal with grease.

3. Position a new gasket on the mating surface of the cylinder block with adhesive.

Installing the rear main oil seal into the oil seal retainer on 1973–74 models

4. Align the dowel holes with the locating dowels and mount the oil seal retainer to the cylinder block.

5. Install the oil pan.

OIL PUMP

Removal and Installation

1. Drain and remove the oil pan or crankcase.

2. Disconnect the oil feed pipe.

3. Remove the two bolts securing the oil pump to the cylinder block and remove the oil pump.

4. Install in the reverse order of removal.

The oil pump on 1974 models; others are very similar

Engine Cooling

RADIATOR

Removal and Installation

1. Drain the radiator by opening the drain cock on the lower part of the radiator.

2. Disconnect the radiator upper and lower hoses.

3. Remove the four bolts retaining the radiator and remove the radiator assembly.

4. Install the radiator in the reverse order of removal.

WATER PUMP

Removal and Installation

1974

1. Disconnect the positive battery cable.

2. Drain the cooling system.

3. Disconnect the upper and lower radiator hoses.

4. Remove the radiator and shroud.

5. Remove the alternator and air pump drive belts.

6. Remove the fan, pulley and spacer.

7. Remove the water pump assembly and gasket.

NOTE: *When removing the water pump, loosen, but do not remove the bolt behind the timing gear cover.*

Loosen, but do not remove the bolt behind the timing gear cover when removing the water pump on 1974 models

8. Remove the radiator lower hose and heater hose at the water pump.

9. Install the water pump in the reverse order of removal, using a new gasket.

1972–73

1. Disconnect the positive battery cable from the battery.

2. Remove the grille.

3. Drain the cooling system.

4. Disconnect the upper and lower radiator hoses.

5. Remove the radiator and shroud.

6. Remove the alternator and air pump belts.

7. Remove the fan, pulley and spacer.

8. Remove the camshaft access cover.

9. Bring the No. 4 piston to TDC of its compression stroke.

10. Remove the crankshaft pulley.

11. Remove the jackshaft access cover.

12. Remove the primary chain tensioner.

13. Remove the upper left and right chain dampener bolts.

14. Remove the camshaft gear bolt and gear.

15. Remove the jackshaft secondary sprocket bolt and remove the sprocket.

16. Remove secondary timing chain.

17. Remove the left chain dampener.

18. Remove the three cylinder head-to-timing cover attaching bolts.

19. Remove the timing case cover bolts.

20. Remove the timing case cover and gasket.

21. Remove the water pump assembly and gasket.

22. Remove the heater hose at the water pump.

23. Install in the reverse order of removal. Use new gaskets on the water pump and the timing covers.

THERMOSTAT

Removal and Installation

1. Drain the radiator by opening the drain petcock on the bottom of the radiator.

2. Disconnect the upper and lower radiator hoses.

3. Disconnect the water outlet from the engine.

4. Remove the thermostat.

5. Replace the thermostat in the reverse order of removal, using a new gasket under the outlet housing and making sure that the thermostat is placed so that the spring end is inside the engine.

Engine Rebuilding

This section describes, in detail, the procedures involved in rebuilding a typical engine. The procedures specifically refer to an inline engine, however, they are basically identical to those used in rebuilding engines of nearly all design and configurations. Procedures for servicing atypical engines (i.e., horizontally opposed) are described in the appropriate section, although in most cases, cylinder head reconditioning procedures described in this chapter will apply.

The section is divided into two sections. The first, Cylinder Head Reconditioning, assumes that the cylinder head is removed from the engine, all manifolds are removed, and the cylinder head is on a workbench. The camshaft should be removed from overhead cam cylinder heads. The second section, Cylinder Block Reconditioning, covers the block, pistons, connecting rods and crankshaft. It is assumed that the engine is mounted on a work stand, and the cylinder head and all accessories are removed.

Procedures are identified as follows:

Unmarked—Basic procedures that must be performed in order to successfully complete the rebuilding process.

Starred (*)—Procedures that should be performed to ensure maximum performance and engine life.

Double starred (**)—Procedures that may be performed to increase engine performance and reliability. These procedures are usually reserved for extremely heavy-duty or competition usage.

In many cases, a choice of methods is also provided. Methods are identified in the same manner as procedures. The choice of method for a procedure is at the discretion of the user.

The tools required for the basic rebuilding procedure should, with minor exceptions, be those

TORQUE (ft. lbs.)*

U.S.

Bolt Diameter (inches)	Bolt Grade (SAE)				Wrench Size (inches)	
	⬡ 1 and 2	⬡ 5	⬡ 6	⬡ 8	Bolt	Nut
1/4	5	7	10	10.5	3/8	7/16
5/16	9	14	19	22	1/2	9/16
3/8	15	25	34	37	9/16	5/8
7/16	24	40	55	60	5/8	3/4
1/2	37	60	85	92	3/4	13/16
9/16	53	88	120	132	7/8	7/8
5/8	74	120	167	180	15/16	1
3/4	120	200	280	296	1-1/8	1-1/8
7/8	190	302	440	473	1-5/16	1-5/16
1	282	466	660	714	1-1/2	1-1/2

Metric

Bolt Diameter (mm)	Bolt Grade				Wrench Size (mm)
	5D 5D	8G 8G	10K 10K	12K 12K	Bolt and Nut
6	5	6	8	10	10
8	10	16	22	27	14
10	19	31	40	49	17
12	34	54	70	86	19
14	55	89	117	137	22
16	83	132	175	208	24
18	111	182	236	283	27
22	182	284	394	464	32
24	261	419	570	689	36

*—Torque values are for lightly oiled bolts. CAUTION: Bolts threaded into aluminum require much less torque.

General Torque Specifications

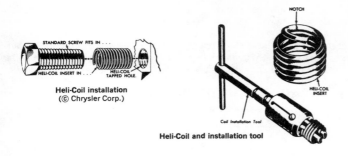

Heli-Coil installation
(© Chrysler Corp.)

Heli-Coil and installation tool

Heli-Coil Insert			Drill	Tap	Insert. Tool	Extracting Tool
Thread Size	Part No.	Insert Length (In.)	Size	Part No.	Part No.	Part No.
1/2 -20	1185-4	3/8	17/64 (.266)	4 CPB	528-4N	1227-6
5/16-18	1185-5	15/32	Q (.332)	5 CPB	528-5N	1227-6
3/8 -16	1185-6	9/16	X (.397)	6 CPB	528-6N	1227-6
7/16-14	1185-7	21/32	29/64 (.453)	7 CPB	528-7N	1227-16
1/2 -13	1185-8	3/4	33/64 (.516)	8 CPB	528-8N	1227-16

Heli-Coil Specifications

included in a mechanic's tool kit. An accurate torque wrench, and a dial indicator (reading in thousandths) mounted on a universal base should be available. Bolts and nuts with no torque specification should be tightened according to size (see chart). Special tools, where required, all are readily available from the major tool suppliers (i.e., Craftsman, Snap-On, K-D). The services of a competent automotive machine shop must also be readily available.

When assembling the engine, any parts that will be in frictional contact must be pre-lubricated, to provide protection on initial start-up. Vortex Pre-Lube, STP, or any product specifically formulated for this purpose may be used. NOTE: *Do not use engine oil.* Where semi-permanent (locked but removable) installation of bolts or nuts is desired, threads should be cleaned and coated with Loctite. Studs may be permanently installed using Loctite Stud and Bearing Mount.

Aluminum has become increasingly popular for use in engines, due to its low weight and excellent heat transfer characteristics. The following precautions

must be observed when handling aluminum engine parts:
—Never hot-tank aluminum parts.
—Remove all aluminum parts (identification tags, etc.) from engine parts before hot-tanking (otherwise they will be removed during the process).
—Always coat threads lightly with engine oil or anti-seize compounds before installation, to prevent seizure.
—Never over-torque bolts or spark plugs in aluminum threads. Should stripping occur, threads can be restored according to the following procedure, using Heli-Coil thread inserts:

Tap drill the hole with the stripped threads to the specified size (see chart). Using the specified tap (NOTE: *Heli-Coil tap sizes refer to the size thread being replaced, rather than the actual tap size*), tap the hole for the Heli-Coil. Place the insert on the proper installation tool (see chart). Apply pressure on the insert while winding it clockwise into the hole, until the top of the insert is one turn below the surface. Remove the installation tool, and break the installation tang from the bottom of the in-

sert by moving it up and down. If the Heli-Coil must be removed, tap the removal tool firmly into the hole, so that it engages the top thread, and turn the tool counter-clockwise to extract the insert.

Snapped bolts or studs may be removed, using a stud extractor (unthreaded) or Vise-Grip pliers (threaded). Penetrating oil (e.g., Liquid Wrench) will often aid in breaking frozen threads. In cases where the stud or bolt is flush with, or below the surface, proceed as follows:

Drill a hole in the broken stud or bolt, approximately ½ its diameter. Select a screw extractor (e.g., Easy-Out) of the proper size, and tap it into the stud or bolt. Turn the extractor counter-clockwise to remove the stud or bolt.

Magnaflux and Zyglo are inspection techniques used to locate material flaws, such as stress cracks. Magnafluxing coats the part with fine magnetic particles, and subjects the part to a magnetic field. Cracks cause breaks

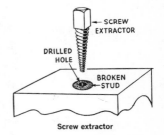

Screw extractor

in the magnetic field, which are outlined by the particles. Since Magnaflux is a magnetic process, it is applicable only to ferrous materials. The Zyglo process coats the material with a fluorescent dye penetrant, and then subjects it to blacklight inspection, under which cracks glow bright-

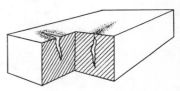

Magnaflux indication of cracks

ly. Parts made of any material may be tested using Zyglo. While Magnaflux and Zyglo are excellent for general inspection, and locating hidden defects, specific checks of suspected cracks may be made at lower cost and more readily using spot check dye. The dye is sprayed onto the suspected area, wiped off, and the area is then sprayed with a developer. Cracks then will show up bright- ly. Spot check dyes will only indicate surface cracks; therefore, structural cracks below the surface may escape detection. When questionable, the part should be tested using Magnaflux or Zyglo.

CYLINDER HEAD RECONDITIONING

Procedure	Method
Identify the valves: 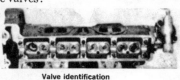 **Valve identification** (© SAAB)	Invert the cylinder head, and number the valve faces front to rear, using a permanent felt-tip marker.
Remove the rocker arms:	Remove the rocker arms with shaft(s) or balls and nuts. Wire the sets of rockers, balls and nuts together, and identify according to the corresponding valve.
Remove the valves and springs:	Using an appropriate valve spring compressor (depending on the configuration of the cylinder head), compress the valve springs. Lift out the keepers with needlenose pliers, release the compressor, and remove the valve, spring, and spring retainer.
Check the valve stem-to-guide clearance:  **Checking the valve stem-to-guide clearance** (© American Motors Corp.)	Clean the valve stem with lacquer thinner or a similar solvent to remove all gum and varnish. Clean the valve guides using solvent and an expanding wire-type valve guide cleaner. Mount a dial indicator so that the stem is at 90° to the valve stem, as close to the valve guide as possible. Move the valve off its seat, and measure the valve guide-to-stem clearance by moving the stem back and forth to actuate the dial indicator. Measure the valve stems using a micrometer, and compare to specifications, to determine whether stem or guide wear is responsible for excessive clearance.
De-carbon the cylinder head and valves:  **Removing carbon from the cylinder head** (© Chevrolet Div. G.M. Corp.)	Chip carbon away from the valve heads, combustion chambers, and ports, using a chisel made of hardwood. Remove the remaining deposits with a stiff wire brush. NOTE: *Ensure that the deposits are actually removed, rather than burnished.*

Procedure	Method
Hot-tank the cylinder head:	Have the cylinder head hot-tanked to remove grease, corrosion, and scale from the water passages. NOTE: *In the case of overhead cam cylinder heads, consult the operator to determine whether the camshaft bearings will be damaged by the caustic solution.*
Degrease the remaining cylinder head parts:	Using solvent (i.e., Gunk), clean the rockers, rocker shaft(s) (where applicable), rocker balls and nuts, springs, spring retainers, and keepers. Do not remove the protective coating from the springs.
Check the cylinder head for warpage: (1)(3) CHECK DIAGONALLY (2) CHECK ACROSS CENTER A 2895-A **Checking the cylinder head for warpage** (© Ford Motor Co.)	Place a straight-edge across the gasket surface of the cylinder head. Using feeler gauges, determine the clearance at the center of the straight-edge. Measure across both diagonals, along the longitudinal centerline, and across the cylinder head at several points. If warpage exceeds .003″ in a 6″ span, or .006″ over the total length, the cylinder head must be resurfaced. NOTE: *If warpage exceeds the manufacturers maximum tolerance for material removal, the cylinder head must be replaced.* When milling the cylinder heads of V-type engines, the intake manifold mounting position is altered, and must be corrected by milling the manifold flange a proportionate amount.
** Porting and gasket matching:	** Coat the manifold flanges of the cylinder head with Prussian blue dye. Glue intake and exhaust gaskets to the cylinder head in their installed position using rubber cement and scribe the outline of the ports on the manifold flanges. Remove the gaskets. Using a small cutter in a hand-held power tool (i.e., Dremel Moto-Tool), gradually taper the walls of the port out to the scribed outline of the gasket. Further enlargement of the ports should include the removal of sharp edges and radiusing of sharp corners. Do not alter the valve guides. NOTE: *The most efficient port configuration is determined only by extensive testing. Therefore, it is best to consult someone experienced with the head in question to determine the optimum alterations.*

Marking the cylinder head for gasket matching
(© Petersen Publishing Co.)

Port configuration before and after gasket matching
(© Petersen Publishing Co.)

Procedure	*Method*
** Polish the ports:	** Using a grinding stone with the above mentioned tool, polish the walls of the intake and exhaust ports, and combustion chamber. Use progressively finer stones until all surface imperfections are removed. NOTE: *Through testing, it has been determined that a smooth surface is more effective than a mirror polished surface in intake ports, and vice-versa in exhaust ports.*

Relieved and polished ports
(© Petersen Publishing Co.)

Polished combustion chamber
(© Petersen Publishing Co.)

* Knurling the valve guides:	* Valve guides which are not excessively worn or distorted may, in some cases, be knurled rather than replaced. Knurling is a process in which metal is displaced and raised, thereby reducing clearance. Knurling also provides excellent oil control. The possibility of knurling rather than replacing valve guides should be discussed with a machinist.

Cut-away view of a knurled valve guide
(© Petersen Publishing Co.)

Replacing the valve guides: NOTE: *Valve guides should only be replaced if damaged or if an oversize valve stem is not available.*	Depending on the type of cylinder head, valve guides may be pressed, hammered, or shrunk in. In cases where the guides are shrunk into the head, replacement should be left to an equipped machine shop. In other cases, the guides are replaced as follows: Press or tap the valve guides out of the head using a stepped drift (see illustration). Determine the height above the boss that the guide must extend, and obtain a stack of washers, their I.D. similar to the guide's O.D., of that height. Place the stack of washers on the guide, and insert the guide into the boss. NOTE: *Valve guides are often tapered or beveled for installation.* Using the stepped installation tool (see illustration), press or tap the guides into position. Ream the guides according to the size of the valve stem.

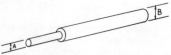

A-VALVE GUIDE I.D.
B-SLIGHTLY SMALLER THAN VALVE GUIDE O.D.

Valve guide removal tool

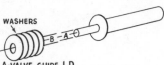

WASHERS

A-VALVE GUIDE I.D.
B-LARGER THAN THE VALVE GUIDE O.D.

Valve guide installation tool (with washers used during installation)

Procedure	Method
Replacing valve seat inserts:	Replacement of valve seat inserts which are worn beyond resurfacing or broken, if feasible, must be done by a machine shop.
Resurfacing (grinding) the valve face:  **Grinding a valve** (© Subaru) 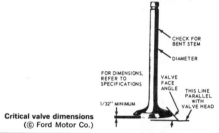 **Critical valve dimensions** (© Ford Motor Co.)	Using a valve grinder, resurface the valves according to specifications. CAUTION: *Valve face angle is not always identical to valve seat angle.* A minimum margin of 1/32″ should remain after grinding the valve. The valve stem tip should also be squared and resurfaced, by placing the stem in the V-block of the grinder, and turning it while pressing lightly against the grinding wheel.
Resurfacing the valve seats using reamers:  **Reaming the valve seat** (© S.p.A. Fiat) **Valve seat width and centering** (© Ford Motor Co.)	Select a reamer of the correct seat angle, slightly larger than the diameter of the valve seat, and assemble it with a pilot of the correct size. Install the pilot into the valve guide, and using steady pressure, turn the reamer clockwise. CAUTION: *Do not turn the reamer counter-clockwise.* Remove only as much material as necessary to clean the seat. Check the concentricity of the seat (see below). If the dye method is not used, coat the valve face with Prussian blue dye, install and rotate it on the valve seat. Using the dye marked area as a centering guide, center and narrow the valve seat to specifications with correction cutters. NOTE: *When no specifications are available, minimum seat width for exhaust valves should be 5/64″, intake valves 1/16″.* After making correction cuts, check the position of the valve seat on the valve face using Prussian blue dye.
* Resurfacing the valve seats using a grinder:  **Grinding a valve seat** (© Subaru)	Select a pilot of the correct size, and a coarse stone of the correct seat angle. Lubricate the pilot if necessary, and install the tool in the valve guide. Move the stone on and off the seat at approximately two cycles per second, until all flaws are removed from the seat. Install a fine stone, and finish the seat. Center and narrow the seat using correction stones, as described above.

Procedure	Method
Checking the valve seat concentricity: 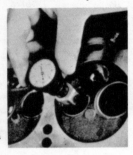 **Checking the valve seat concentricity using a dial gauge** (© American Motors Corp.)	Coat the valve face with Prussian blue dye, install the valve, and rotate it on the valve seat. If the entire seat becomes coated, and the valve is known to be concentric, the seat is concentric.
	* Install the dial gauge pilot into the guide, and rest the arm on the valve seat. Zero the gauge, and rotate the arm around the seat. Run-out should not exceed .002".
* Lapping the valves: NOTE: *Valve lapping is done to ensure efficient sealing of resurfaced valves and seats. Valve lapping alone is not recommended for use as a resurfacing procedure.*  **Hand lapping the valves** HAND DRILL ROD SUCTION CUP **Home made mechanical valve lapping tool**	* Invert the cylinder head, lightly lubricate the valve stems, and install the valves in the head as numbered. Coat valve seats with fine grinding compound, and attach the lapping tool suction cup to a valve head (NOTE: *Moisten the suction cup*). Rotate the tool between the palms, changing position and lifting the tool often to prevent grooving. Lap the valve until a smooth, polished seat is evident. Remove the valve and tool, and rinse away all traces of grinding compound.
	** Fasten a suction cup to a piece of drill rod, and mount the rod in a hand drill. Proceed as above, using the hand drill as a lapping tool. CAUTION: *Due to the higher speeds involved when using the hand drill, care must be exercised to avoid grooving the seat.* Lift the tool and change direction of rotation often.
Check the valve springs:  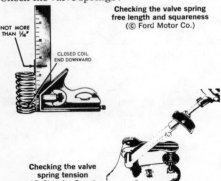 **Checking the valve spring free length and squareness** (© Ford Motor Co.) NOT MORE THAN 1/16" CLOSED COIL END DOWNWARD **Checking the valve spring tension** (© Chrysler Corp.)	Place the spring on a flat surface next to a square. Measure the height of the spring, and rotate it against the edge of the square to measure distortion. If spring height varies (by comparison) by more than 1/16" or if distortion exceeds 1/16", replace the spring.
	** In addition to evaluating the spring as above, test the spring pressure at the installed and compressed (installed height minus valve lift) height using a valve spring tester. Springs used on small displacement engines (up to 3 liters) should be ± 1 lb. of all other springs in either position. A tolerance of ± 5 lbs. is permissible on larger engines.

Procedure	Method
* Install valve stem seals:  **Valve stem seal installation** (© Ford Motor Co.) SEAL	* Due to the pressure differential that exists at the ends of the intake valve guides (atmospheric pressure above, manifold vacuum below), oil is drawn through the valve guides into the intake port. This has been alleviated somewhat since the addition of positive crankcase ventilation, which lowers the pressure above the guides. Several types of valve stem seals are available to reduce blow-by. Certain seals simply slip over the stem and guide boss, while others require that the boss be machined. Recently, Teflon guide seals have become popular. Consult a parts supplier or machinist concerning availability and suggested usages. NOTE: *When installing seals, ensure that a small amount of oil is able to pass the seal to lubricate the valve guides; otherwise, excessive wear may result.*
Install the valves:	Lubricate the valve stems, and install the valves in the cylinder head as numbered. Lubricate and position the seals (if used, see above) and the valve springs. Install the spring retainers, compress the springs, and insert the keys using needlenose pliers or a tool designed for this purpose. NOTE: *Retain the keys with wheel bearing grease during installation.*
Checking valve spring installed height: 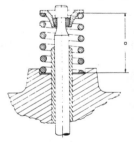  **Valve spring installed height dimension** (© Porsche) **Measuring valve spring installed height** (© Petersen Publishing Co.)	Measure the distance between the spring pad and the lower edge of the spring retainer, and compare to specifications. If the installed height is incorrect, add shim washers between the spring pad and the spring. CAUTION: *Use only washers designed for this purpose.*
** CC'ing the combustion chambers:	** Invert the cylinder head and place a bead of sealer around a combustion chamber. Install an apparatus designed for this purpose (burette mounted on a clear plate; see illustration) over the combustion chamber, and fill with the specified fluid to an even mark on the burette. Record the burette reading, and fill the combustion chamber with fluid. (NOTE: *A hole drilled in the plate will permit air to escape*). Subtract the burette reading, with the combustion chamber filled, from the previous reading, to determine combustion chamber volume in cc's. Duplicate this procedure in all combustion

Procedure	*Method*

CC'ing the combustion chamber
(© Petersen Publishing Co.)

chambers on the cylinder head, and compare the readings. The volume of all combustion chambers should be made equal to that of the largest. Combustion chamber volume may be increased in two ways. When only a small change is required (usually), a small cutter or coarse stone may be used to remove material from the combustion chamber. NOTE: *Check volume frequently.* Remove material over a wide area, so as not to change the configuration of the combustion chamber. When a larger change is required, the valve seat may be sunk (lowered into the head). NOTE: *When altering valve seat, remember to compensate for the change in spring installed height.*

Inspect the rocker arms, balls, studs, and nuts (where applicable):

Stress cracks in rocker nuts
(© Ford Motor Co.)

Visually inspect the rocker arms, balls, studs, and nuts for cracks, galling, burning, scoring, or wear. If all parts are intact, liberally lubricate the rocker arms and balls, and install them on the cylinder head. If wear is noted on a rocker arm at the point of valve contact, grind it smooth and square, removing as little material as possible. Replace the rocker arm if excessively worn. If a rocker stud shows signs of wear, it must be replaced (see below). If a rocker nut shows stress cracks, replace it. If an exhaust ball is galled or burned, substitute the intake ball from the same cylinder (if it is intact), and install a new intake ball. NOTE: *Avoid using new rocker balls on exhaust valves.*

Replacing rocker studs:

Reaming the stud bore for oversize rocker studs
(© Buick Div. G.M. Corp.)

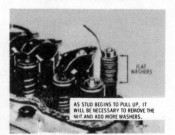

Extracting a pressed in rocker stud
(© Buick Div. G.M. Corp.)

AS STUD BEGINS TO PULL UP, IT WILL BE NECESSARY TO REMOVE THE NUT AND ADD MORE WASHERS.

In order to remove a threaded stud, lock two nuts on the stud, and unscrew the stud using the lower nut. Coat the lower threads of the new stud with Loctite, and install.

Two alternative methods are available for replacing pressed in studs. Remove the damaged stud using a stack of washers and a nut (see illustration). In the first, the boss is reamed .005-.006″ oversize, and an oversize stud pressed in. Control the stud extension over the boss using washers, in the same manner as valve guides. Before installing the stud, coat it with white lead and grease. To retain the stud more positively, drill a hole through the stud and boss, and install a roll pin. In the second method, the boss is tapped, and a threaded stud installed. Retain the stud using Loctite Stud and Bearing Mount.

Procedure	*Method*
Inspect the rocker shaft(s) and rocker arms (where applicable):  **Disassembled rocker shaft parts arranged for inspection** (© American Motors Corp.) 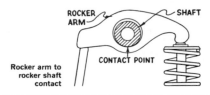 **Rocker arm to rocker shaft contact**	Remove rocker arms, springs and washers from rocker shaft. NOTE: *Lay out parts in the order they are removed.* Inspect rocker arms for pitting or wear on the valve contact point, or excessive bushing wear. Bushings need only be replaced if wear is excessive, because the rocker arm normally contacts the shaft at one point only. Grind the valve contact point of rocker arm smooth if necessary, removing as little material as possible. If excessive material must be removed to smooth and square the arm, it should be replaced. Clean out all oil holes and passages in rocker shaft. If shaft is grooved or worn, replace it. Lubricate and assemble the rocker shaft.
Inspect the camshaft bushings and the camshaft (overhead cam engines):	See next section.
Inspect the pushrods:	Remove the pushrods, and, if hollow, clean out the oil passages using fine wire. Roll each pushrod over a piece of clean glass. If a distinct clicking sound is heard as the pushrod rolls, the rod is bent, and must be replaced.
	✻ The length of all pushrods must be equal. Measure the length of the pushrods, compare to specifications, and replace as necessary.
Inspect the valve lifters: 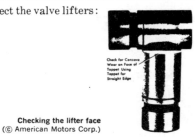 Check for Concave Wear on Face of Tappet Using Tappet for Straight Edge **Checking the lifter face** (© American Motors Corp.)	Remove lifters from their bores, and remove gum and varnish, using solvent. Clean walls of lifter bores. Check lifters for concave wear as illustrated. If face is worn concave, replace lifter, and carefully inspect the camshaft. Lightly lubricate lifter and insert it into its bore. If play is excessive, an oversize lifter must be installed (where possible). Consult a machinist concerning feasibility. If play is satisfactory, remove, lubricate, and reinstall the lifter.
✻ Testing hydraulic lifter leak down: 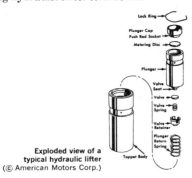 Lock Ring Plunger Cap Push Rod Socket Metering Disc Plunger Valve Seat Valve Valve Spring Valve Retainer Plunger Return Spring Tappet Body **Exploded view of a typical hydraulic lifter** (© American Motors Corp.)	Submerge lifter in a container of kerosene. Chuck a used pushrod or its equivalent into a drill press. Position container of kerosene so pushrod acts on the lifter plunger. Pump lifter with the drill press, until resistance increases. Pump several more times to bleed any air out of lifter. Apply very firm, constant pressure to the lifter, and observe rate at which fluid bleeds out of lifter. If the fluid bleeds very quickly (less than 15 seconds), lifter is defective. If the time exceeds 60 seconds, lifter is sticking. In either case, recondition or replace lifter. If lifter is operating properly (leak down time 15-60 seconds), lubricate and install it.

CYLINDER BLOCK RECONDITIONING

Procedure	Method
Checking the main bearing clearance:  **Plastigage installed on main bearing journal** (© Chevrolet Div. G.M. Corp.)  **Measuring Plastigage to determine main bearing clearance** (© Chevrolet Div. G.M. Corp.)  **Causes of bearing failure** (© Ford Motor Co.)	Invert engine, and remove cap from the bearing to be checked. Using a clean, dry rag, thoroughly clean all oil from crankshaft journal and bearing insert. NOTE: *Plastigage is soluble in oil; therefore, oil on the journal or bearing could result in erroneous readings.* Place a piece of Plastigage along the full length of journal, reinstall cap, and torque to specifications. Remove bearing cap, and determine bearing clearance by comparing width of Plastigage to the scale on Plastigage envelope. Journal taper is determined by comparing width of the Plastigage strip near its ends. Rotate crankshaft 90° and retest, to determine journal eccentricity. NOTE: *Do not rotate crankshaft with Plastigage installed.* If bearing insert and journal appear intact, and are within tolerances, no further main bearing service is required. If bearing or journal appear defective, cause of failure should be determined before replacement.

* Remove crankshaft from block (see below). Measure the main bearing journals at each end twice (90° apart) using a micrometer, to determine diameter, journal taper and eccentricity. If journals are within tolerances, reinstall bearing caps at their specified torque. Using a telescope gauge and micrometer, measure bearing I.D. parallel to piston axis and at 30° on each side of piston axis. Subtract journal O.D. from bearing I.D. to determine oil clearance. If crankshaft journals appear defective, or do not meet tolerances, there is no need to measure bearings; for the crankshaft will require grinding and/or undersize bearings will be required. If bearing appears defective, cause for failure should be determined prior to replacement.

Procedure	Method
Checking the connecting rod bearing clearance:  **Plastigage installed on connecting rod bearing journal** (© Chevrolet Div. G.M. Corp.)	Connecting rod bearing clearance is checked in the same manner as main bearing clearance, using Plastigage. Before removing the crankshaft, connecting rod side clearance also should be measured and recorded.

* Checking connecting rod bearing clearance, using a micrometer, is identical to checking main bearing clearance. If no other service

Procedure	Method

Measuring Plastigage to determine connecting rod bearing clearance
(© Chevrolet Div. G.M. Corp.)

is required, the piston and rod assemblies need not be removed.

Removing the crankshaft:

Connecting rod matching marks
(© Ford Motor Co.)

Using a punch, mark the corresponding main bearing caps and saddles according to position (i.e., one punch on the front main cap and saddle, two on the second, three on the third, etc.). Using number stamps, identify the corresponding connecting rods and caps, according to cylinder (if no numbers are present). Remove the main and connecting rod caps, and place sleeves of plastic tubing over the connecting rod bolts, to protect the journals as the crankshaft is removed. Lift the crankshaft out of the block.

Remove the ridge from the top of the cylinder:

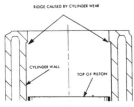

RIDGE CAUSED BY CYLINDER WEAR

CYLINDER WALL   TOP OF PISTON

Cylinder bore ridge
(© Pontiac Div. G.M. Corp.)

In order to facilitate removal of the piston and connecting rod, the ridge at the top of the cylinder (unworn area; see illustration) must be removed. Place the piston at the bottom of the bore, and cover it with a rag. Cut the ridge away using a ridge reamer, exercising extreme care to avoid cutting too deeply. Remove the rag, and remove cuttings that remain on the piston. CAUTION: *If the ridge is not removed, and new rings are installed, damage to rings will result.*

Removing the piston and connecting rod:

Removing the piston
(© SAAB)

Invert the engine, and push the pistons and connecting rods out of the cylinders. If necessary, tap the connecting rod boss with a wooden hammer handle, to force the piston out. CAUTION: *Do not attempt to force the piston past the cylinder ridge* (see above).

Procedure	Method
Service the crankshaft:	Ensure that all oil holes and passages in the crankshaft are open and free of sludge. If necessary, have the crankshaft ground to the largest possible undersize.
	** Have the crankshaft Magnafluxed, to locate stress cracks. Consult a machinist concerning additional service procedures, such as surface hardening (e.g., nitriding, Tuftriding) to improve wear characteristics, cross drilling and chamfering the oil holes to improve lubrication, and balancing.
Removing freeze plugs:	Drill a hole in the center of the freeze plugs, and pry them out using a screwdriver or drift.
Remove the oil gallery plugs:	Threaded plugs should be removed using an appropriate (usually square) wrench. To remove soft, pressed in plugs, drill a hole in the plug, and thread in a sheet metal screw. Pull the plug out by the screw using pliers.
Hot-tank the block:	Have the block hot-tanked to remove grease, corrosion, and scale from the water jackets. NOTE: *Consult the operator to determine whether the camshaft bearings will be damaged during the hot-tank process.*
Check the block for cracks:	Visually inspect the block for cracks or chips. The most common locations are as follows: Adjacent to freeze plugs. Between the cylinders and water jackets. Adjacent to the main bearing saddles. At the extreme bottom of the cylinders. Check only suspected cracks using spot check dye (see introduction). If a crack is located, consult a machinist concerning possible repairs.
	** Magnaflux the block to locate hidden cracks. If cracks are located, consult a machinist about feasibility of repair.
Install the oil gallery plugs and freeze plugs:	Coat freeze plugs with sealer and tap into position using a piece of pipe, slightly smaller than the plug, as a driver. To ensure retention, stake the edges of the plugs. Coat threaded oil gallery plugs with sealer and install. Drive replacement soft plugs into block using a large drift as a driver.
	* Rather than reinstalling lead plugs, drill and tap the holes, and install threaded plugs.

Procedure	*Method*

Check the bore diameter and surface:

Visually inspect the cylinder bores for roughness, scoring, or scuffing. If evident, the cylinder bore must be bored or honed oversize to eliminate imperfections, and the smallest possible oversize piston used. The new pistons should be given to the machinist with the block, so that the cylinders can be bored or honed exactly to the piston size (plus clearance). If no flaws are evident, measure the bore diameter using a telescope gauge and micrometer, or dial gauge, parallel and perpendicular to the engine centerline, at the top (below the ridge) and bottom of the bore. Subtract the bottom measurements from the top to determine taper, and the parallel to the centerline measurements from the perpendicular measurements to determine eccentricity. If the measurements are not within specifications, the cylinder must be bored or honed, and an oversize piston installed. If the measurements are within specifications the cylinder may be used as is, with only finish honing (see below). NOTE: *Prior to submitting the block for boring, perform the following operation(s).*

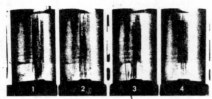

1, 2, 3 Piston skirt seizure resulted in this pattern. Engine must be rebored

4. Piston skirt and oil ring seizure caused this damage. Engine must be rebored

5, 6 Score marks caused by a split piston skirt. Damage is not serious enough to warrant reboring

7. Ring seized longitudinally, causing a score mark 1 3/16" wide, on the land side of the piston groove. The honing pattern is destroyed and the cylinder must be rebored

8. Result of oil ring seizure. Engine must be rebored

9. Oil ring seizure here was not serious enough to warrant reboring. The honing marks are still visible

Cylinder wall damage
(© Daimler-Benz A.G.)

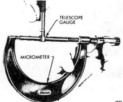

Cylinder bore measuring positions
(© Ford Motor Co.)

Measuring the cylinder bore with a telescope gauge
(© Buick Div. G.M. Corp.)

Determining the cylinder bore by measuring the telescope gauge with a micrometer
(© Buick Div. G.M. Corp.)

Measuring the cylinder bore with a dial gauge
(© Chevrolet Div. G.M. Corp.)

Procedure	Method
Check the block deck for warpage:	Using a straightedge and feeler gauges, check the block deck for warpage in the same manner that the cylinder head is checked (see Cylinder Head Reconditioning). If warpage exceeds specifications, have the deck resurfaced. NOTE: *In certain cases a specification for total material removal (Cylinder head and block deck) is provided. This specification must not be exceeded.*
* Check the deck height:	The deck height is the distance from the crankshaft centerline to the block deck. To measure, invert the engine, and install the crankshaft, retaining it with the center main cap. Measure the distance from the crankshaft journal to the block deck, parallel to the cylinder centerline. Measure the diameter of the end (front and rear) main journals, parallel to the centerline of the cylinders, divide the diameter in half, and subtract it from the previous measurement. The results of the front and rear measurements should be identical. If the difference exceeds .005″, the deck height should be corrected. NOTE: *Block deck height and warpage should be corrected concurrently.*
Check the cylinder block bearing alignment:  Checking main bearing saddle alignment (© Petersen Publishing Co.)	Remove the upper bearing inserts. Place a straightedge in the bearing saddles along the centerline of the crankshaft. If clearance exists between the straightedge and the center saddle, the block must be align-bored.
Clean and inspect the pistons and connecting rods:  Removing the piston rings (© Subaru)	Using a ring expander, remove the rings from the piston. Remove the retaining rings (if so equipped) and remove piston pin. NOTE: *If the piston pin must be pressed out, determine the proper method and use the proper tools; otherwise the piston will distort.* Clean the ring grooves using an appropriate tool, exercising care to avoid cutting too deeply. Thoroughly clean all carbon and varnish from the piston with solvent. CAUTION: *Do not use a wire brush or caustic solvent on pistons.* Inspect the pistons for scuffing, scoring, cracks, pitting, or excessive ring groove wear. If wear is evident, the piston must be replaced. Check the connecting rod length by measuring the rod from the inside of the large end to the inside of the small end using calipers (see

Procedure	*Method*

Cleaning the piston ring grooves
(© Ford Motor Co.)

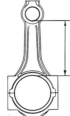

Connecting rod
length checking
dimension

illustration). All connecting rods should be equal length. Replace any rod that differs from the others in the engine.

* Have the connecting rod alignment checked in an alignment fixture by a machinist. Replace any twisted or bent rods.

* Magnaflux the connecting rods to locate stress cracks. If cracks are found, replace the connecting rod.

Fit the pistons to the cylinders:

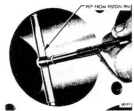

Measuring the cylinder
with a telescope gauge
for piston fitting
(© Buick Div.
G.M. Corp.)

Measuring the piston
for fitting
(© Buick Div.
G.M. Corp.)

Using a telescope gauge and micrometer, or a dial gauge, measure the cylinder bore diameter perpendicular to the piston pin, 2½″ below the deck. Measure the piston perpendicular to its pin on the skirt. The difference between the two measurements is the piston clearance. If the clearance is within specifications or slightly below (after boring or honing), finish honing is all that is required. If the clearance is excessive, try to obtain a slightly larger piston to bring clearance within specifications. Where this is not possible, obtain the first oversize piston, and hone (or if necessary, bore) the cylinder to size.

Assemble the pistons and connecting rods:

Installing piston pin lock rings
(© Nissan Motor Co., Ltd.)

Inspect piston pin, connecting rod small end bushing, and piston bore for galling, scoring, or excessive wear. If evident, replace defective part(s). Measure the I.D. of the piston boss and connecting rod small end, and the O.D. of the piston pin. If within specifications, assemble piston pin and rod. CAUTION: *If piston pin must be pressed in, determine the proper method and use the proper tools; otherwise the piston will distort.* Install the lock rings; ensure that they seat properly. If the parts are not within specifications, determine the service method for the type of engine. In some cases, piston and pin are serviced as an assembly when either is defective. Others specify reaming the piston and connecting rods for an oversize pin. If the connecting rod bushing is worn, it may in many cases be replaced. Reaming the piston and replacing the rod bushing are machine shop operations.

Procedure	*Method*
Clean and inspect the camshaft: 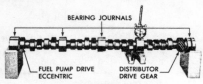 **Checking the camshaft for straightness** (© Chevrolet Motor Div. G.M. Corp.) 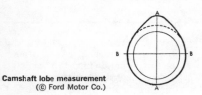 **Camshaft lobe measurement** (© Ford Motor Co.)	Degrease the camshaft, using solvent, and clean out all oil holes. Visually inspect cam lobes and bearing journals for excessive wear. If a lobe is questionable, check all lobes as indicated below. If a journal or lobe is worn, the camshaft must be reground or replaced. NOTE: *If a journal is worn, there is a good chance that the bushings are worn.* If lobes and journals appear intact, place the front and rear journals in V-blocks, and rest a dial indicator on the center journal. Rotate the camshaft to check straightness. If deviation exceeds .001″, replace the camshaft.
	* Check the camshaft lobes with a micrometer, by measuring the lobes from the nose to base and again at 90° (see illustration). The lift is determined by subtracting the second measurement from the first. If all exhaust lobes and all intake lobes are not identical, the camshaft must be reground or replaced.
Replace the camshaft bearings: 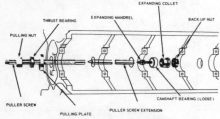 **Camshaft removal and installation tool (typical)** (© Ford Motor Co.)	If excessive wear is indicated, or if the engine is being completely rebuilt, camshaft bearings should be replaced as follows: Drive the camshaft rear plug from the block. Assemble the removal puller with its shoulder on the bearing to be removed. Gradually tighten the puller nut until bearing is removed. Remove remaining bearings, leaving the front and rear for last. To remove front and rear bearings, reverse position of the tool, so as to pull the bearings in toward the center of the block. Leave the tool in this position, pilot the new front and rear bearings on the installer, and pull them into position. Return the tool to its original position and pull remaining bearings into position. NOTE: *Ensure that oil holes align when installing bearings.* Replace camshaft rear plug, and stake it into position to aid retention.
Finish hone the cylinders: 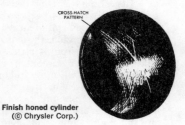 **Finish honed cylinder** (© Chrysler Corp.)	Chuck a flexible drive hone into a power drill, and insert it into the cylinder. Start the hone, and move it up and down in the cylinder at a rate which will produce approximately a 60° cross-hatch pattern (see illustration). NOTE: *Do not extend the hone below the cylinder bore.* After developing the pattern, remove the hone and recheck piston fit. Wash the cylinders with a detergent and water solution to remove abrasive dust, dry, and wipe several times with a rag soaked in engine oil.

Procedure	*Method*
Check piston ring end-gap:	Compress the piston rings to be used in a cylinder, one at a time, into that cylinder, and press them approximately 1″ below the deck with an inverted piston. Using feeler gauges, measure the ring end-gap, and compare to specifications. Pull the ring out of the cylinder and file the ends with a fine file to obtain proper clearance. CAUTION: *If inadequate ring end-gap is utilized, ring breakage will result.*

Checking ring end-gap
(© Chevrolet Motor Div. G.M. Corp.)

Install the piston rings:	Inspect the ring grooves in the piston for excessive wear or taper. If necessary, recut the groove(s) for use with an overwidth ring or a standard ring and spacer. If the groove is worn uniformly, overwidth rings, or standard rings and spacers may be installed without recutting. Roll the outside of the ring around the groove to check for burrs or deposits. If any are found, remove with a fine file. Hold the ring in the groove, and measure side clearance. If necessary, correct as indicated above. NOTE: *Always install any additional spacers above the piston ring.* The ring groove must be deep enough to allow the ring to seat below the lands (see illustration). In many cases, a "go-no-go" depth gauge will be provided with the piston rings. Shallow grooves may be corrected by recutting, while deep grooves require some type of filler or expander behind the piston. Consult the piston ring supplier concerning the suggested method. Install the rings on the piston, lowest ring first, using a ring expander. NOTE: *Position the ring markings as specified by the manufacturer (see car section).*

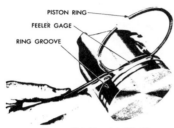

Checking ring side clearance
(© Chrysler Corp.)

  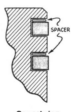

CORRECT   INCORRECT   Correct ring
Piston groove depth   spacer installation

Install the camshaft:	Liberally lubricate the camshaft lobes and journals, and slide the camshaft into the block. CAUTION: *Exercise extreme care to avoid damaging the bearings when inserting the camshaft.* Install and tighten the camshaft thrust plate retaining bolts.

Check camshaft end-play:	Using feeler gauges, determine whether the clearance between the camshaft boss (or gear) and backing plate is within specifications. Install shims behind the thrust plate, or reposition the camshaft gear and retest end-play.

Checking camshaft
end-play with a
feeler gauge
(© Ford Motor Co.)

Procedure	*Method*

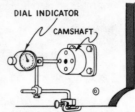

DIAL INDICATOR

CAMSHAFT

Checking camshaft end-play with a dial indicator

* Mount a dial indicator stand so that the stem of the dial indicator rests on the nose of the camshaft, parallel to the camshaft axis. Push the camshaft as far in as possible and zero the gauge. Move the camshaft outward to determine the amount of camshaft end-play. If the end-play is not within tolerance, install shims behind the thrust plate, or reposition the camshaft gear and retest.

Install the rear main seal (where applicable):

Seating the rear main seal
(© Buick Div. G.M. Corp.)

Position the block with the bearing saddles facing upward. Lay the rear main seal in its groove and press it lightly into its seat. Place a piece of pipe the same diameter as the crankshaft journal into the saddle, and firmly seat the seal. Hold the pipe in position, and trim the ends of the seal flush if required.

Install the crankshaft:

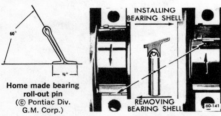

60°

Home made bearing roll-out pin
(© Pontiac Div. G.M. Corp.)

INSTALLING BEARING SHELL

REMOVING BEARING SHELL

Removal and installation of upper bearing insert using a roll-out pin
(© Buick Div. G.M. Corp.)

Thoroughly clean the main bearing saddles and caps. Place the upper halves of the bearing inserts on the saddles and press into position. NOTE: *Ensure that the oil holes align.* Press the corresponding bearing inserts into the main bearing caps. Lubricate the upper main bearings, and lay the crankshaft in position. Place a strip of Plastigage on each of the crankshaft journals, install the main caps, and torque to specifications. Remove the main caps, and compare the Plastigage to the scale on the Plastigage envelope. If clearances are within tolerances, remove the Plastigage, turn the crankshaft 90°, wipe off all oil and retest. If all clearances are correct, remove all Plastigage, thoroughly

PRY FORWARD

THRUST BEARING

PRY CRANKSHAFT FORWARD

HOLD CRANKSHAFT FORWARD

PRY CAP BACKWARD

THRUST BEARING

PRY CAP BACKWARD

THRUST BEARING

HOLD CRANKSHAFT FORWARD

TIGHTEN CAP

A2879-A

Aligning the thrust bearing
(© Ford Motor Co.)

Procedure	Method
	lubricate the main caps and bearing journals, and install the main caps. If clearances are not within tolerance, the upper bearing inserts may be removed, without removing the crankshaft, using a bearing roll out pin (see illustration). Roll in a bearing that will provide proper clearance, and retest. Torque all main caps, excluding the thrust bearing cap, to specifications. Tighten the thrust bearing cap finger tight. To properly align the thrust bearing, pry the crankshaft the extent of its axial travel several times, the last movement held toward the front of the engine, and torque the thrust bearing cap to specifications. Determine the crankshaft end-play (see below), and bring within tolerance with thrust washers.
Measure crankshaft end-play:  **Checking crankshaft end-play with a dial indicator** (© Ford Motor Co.) A 2908-A  **Checking crankshaft end-play with a feeler gauge** (© Chevrolet Div. (G.M. Corp.)	Mount a dial indicator stand on the front of the block, with the dial indicator stem resting on the nose of the crankshaft, parallel to the crankshaft axis. Pry the crankshaft the extent of its travel rearward, and zero the indicator. Pry the crankshaft forward and record crankshaft end-play. NOTE: *Crankshaft end-play also may be measured at the thrust bearing, using feeler gauges* (see illustration).
Install the pistons:	Press the upper connecting rod bearing halves into the connecting rods, and the lower halves into the connecting rod caps. Position the piston ring gaps according to specifications (see car section), and lubricate the pistons. Install a ring compresser on a piston, and press two long (8″) pieces of plastic tubing over the rod bolts. Using the plastic tubes as a guide, press the pistons into the bores and onto the crankshaft with a wooden hammer handle. After seating the rod on the crankshaft journal, remove the tubes and install the cap finger tight. Install the remaining pistons in the same man-

Procedure	*Method*

Tubing used as guide when installing
a piston
(© Oldsmobile Div. G.M. Corp.)

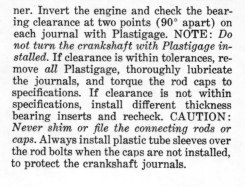

ner. Invert the engine and check the bearing clearance at two points (90° apart) on each journal with Plastigage. NOTE: *Do not turn the crankshaft with Plastigage installed.* If clearance is within tolerances, remove *all* Plastigage, thoroughly lubricate the journals, and torque the rod caps to specifications. If clearance is not within specifications, install different thickness bearing inserts and recheck. CAUTION: *Never shim or file the connecting rods or caps.* Always install plastic tube sleeves over the rod bolts when the caps are not installed, to protect the crankshaft journals.

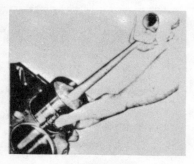

Installing a piston
(© Chevrolet Div. G.M. Corp.)

Check connecting rod side clearance:

Determine the clearance between the sides of the connecting rods and the crankshaft, using feeler gauges. If clearance is below the minimum tolerance, the rod may be machined to provide adequate clearance. If clearance is excessive, substitute an unworn rod, and recheck. If clearance is still outside specifications, the crankshaft must be welded and reground, or replaced.

Checking connecting rod side clearance
(© Chevrolet Div. G.M. Corp.)

Inspect the timing chain:

Visually inspect the timing chain for broken or loose links, and replace the chain if any are found. If the chain will flex sideways, it must be replaced. Install the timing chain as specified. NOTE: *If the original timing chain is to be reused, install it in its original position.*

Procedure	Method
Check timing gear backlash and runout:  Checking camshaft gear backlash (© Chevrolet Div. G.M. Corp.)  Checking camshaft gear runout (© Chevrolet Div. G.M. Corp.)	Mount a dial indicator with its stem resting on a tooth of the camshaft gear (as illustrated). Rotate the gear until all slack is removed, and zero the indicator. Rotate the gear in the opposite direction until slack is removed, and record gear backlash. Mount the indicator with its stem resting on the edge of the camshaft gear, parallel to the axis of the camshaft. Zero the indicator, and turn the camshaft gear one full turn, recording the runout. If either backlash or runout exceed specifications, replace the worn gear(s).

Completing the Rebuilding Process

Following the above procedures, complete the rebuilding process as follows:

Fill the oil pump with oil, to prevent cavitating (sucking air) on initial engine start up. Install the oil pump and the pickup tube on the engine. Coat the oil pan gasket as necessary, and install the gasket and the oil pan. Mount the flywheel and the crankshaft vibrational damper or pulley on the crankshaft. NOTE: *Always use new bolts when installing the flywheel.* Inspect the clutch shaft pilot bushing in the crankshaft. If the bushing is excessively worn, remove it with an expanding puller and a slide hammer, and tap a new bushing into place.

Position the engine, cylinder head side up. Lubricate the lifters, and install them into their bores. Install the cylinder head, and torque it as specified in the car section. Insert the pushrods (where applicable), and install the rocker shaft(s) (if so equipped) or position the rocker arms on the pushrods. If solid lifters are utilized, adjust the valves to the "cold" specifications.

Mount the intake and exhaust manifolds, the carburetor(s), the distributor and spark plugs. Adjust the point gap and the static ignition timing. Mount all accessories and install the engine in the car. Fill the radiator with coolant, and the crankcase with high quality engine oil.

Break-in Procedure

Start the engine, and allow it to run at low speed for a few minutes, while checking for leaks. Stop the engine, check the oil level, and fill as necessary. Restart the engine, and fill the cooling system to capacity. Check the point dwell angle and adjust the ignition timing and the valves. Run the engine at low to medium speed (800-2500 rpm) for approximately ½ hour, and retorque the cylinder head bolts. Road test the car, and check again for leaks.

Follow the manufacturer's recommended engine break-in procedure and maintenance schedule for new engines.

4 · Emission Controls and Fuel System

Emission Controls

There are three types of automotive pollutants; crankcase fumes, exhaust gases and gasoline evaporation. The equipment that is used to limit these pollutants is commonly called emission control equipment.

CRANKCASE EMISSION CONTROLS

The crankcase emission control equipment consists of a positive crankcase ventilation valve (PCV), a closed or open oil filler cap and hoses to connect this equipment.

When the engine is running, a small portion of the gases which are formed in the combustion chamber during combustion leak by the piston rings and enter the crankcase. Since these gases are under pressure they tend to escape from the crankcase and enter into the atmosphere. If these gases were allowed to remain in the crankcase for any length of time, they would contaminate the engine oil and cause sludge to build up. If the gases are allowed to escape into the atmosphere, they would pollute the air, as they contain unburned hydrocarbons. The crankcase emission control equipment recycles these gases back into

the engine combustion chamber where they are burned.

Crankcase gases are recycled in the following manner: while the engine is running, clean filtered air is drawn into the crankcase through the carburetor air filter and then through a hose leading to the rocker cover. As the air passes through the crankcase it picks up the combustion gases and carries them out of the crankcase, up through the PCV valve and into the intake manifold. After they enter the intake manifold they are drawn into the combustion chamber and burned.

The most critical component in the system is the PCV valve. This vacuum controlled valve regulates the amount of gases which are recycled into the combustion chamber. At low engine speeds the valve is partially closed, limiting the flow of gases into the intake manifold. As engine speed increases, the valve opens to admit greater quantities of the gases into the intake manifold. If the valve should become blocked or plugged, the gases will be prevented from escaping from the crankcases by the normal route. Since these gases are under pressure, they will find their own way out of the crankcase. This alternate route is usually a weak oil seal or gasket in the engine. As the gas escapes by the gasket, it also creates an oil leak. Besides causing oil leaks, a clogged PCV valve also allows these gases to remain in the crankcase for an extended period of time, promoting the formation of sludge in the engine.

The above explanation and the troubleshooting procedure which follows applies to all engines with PCV systems.

Testing

Check the PCV system hoses and connections, to see that there are no leaks; then replace or tighten, as necessary.

To check the valve, remove it and blow through both of its ends (as illustrated). When blowing from the side which goes toward the intake manifold, very little air should pass through it. When blowing from the crankcase (valve cover) side, air should pass through freely.

Replace the valve with a new one, if the valve fails to function as outlined.

NOTE: *Do not attempt to clean or adjust the valve; replace it with a new one.*

Removal and Installation

To remove the PCV valve, simply loosen the hose clamp and remove the valve from the manifold-to-crankcase hose and intake manifold. Install the PCV valve in the reverse order of removal.

EVAPORATIVE EMISSION CONTROL SYSTEM

When raw fuel evaporates, the vapors contain hydrocarbons. To prevent these nasties from escaping into the atmosphere, the fuel evaporative emission control system was developed.

The system consists of a sealed fuel tank, a vapor separator tank, check and relief valve and the hoses connecting these components, in the above order leading from the fuel tank, to the crankcase of the engine.

In operation, the vapor formed in the fuel tank passes through the vapor separator, which allows liquid fuel to flow back into fuel tank while allowing fuel vapor to pass onto the check and relief valve and the crankcase. When the engine is not running, if the fuel vapor pressure in the vapor separator becomes as high as 1 to 1.4 in. Hg, the check valve opens and allows the vapor to enter the engine crankcase. Otherwise the check valve is closed to the vapor separator while the engine is not running. When the engine is running, and a vacuum is developed in the fuel tank or in the engine crankcase and the difference of pressure between the relief side and the fuel tank or crankcase becomes 2 in. Hg, the relief valve opens and allows ambient air from the air cleaner into the fuel tank or the engine crankcase. This ambient air replaces the vapor within the fuel tank or crankcase, bringing the fuel tank or crankcase back into a neutral or positive pressure range.

Inspection and Service

Check the hoses for proper connections and damage. Replace as necessary. Check the vapor separator tank for fuel leaks, distortion and dents, and replace as necessary.

Remove the check valve and inspect it for leakage by blowing air into the ports in the check valve. When air is applied from the fuel tank side, the check valve is normal if air passes into the check side (crankcase side), but not leaking into the relief side (air cleaner side). When air is applied from the check side, the valve is normal if the passage of air is restricted. When air is applied from the relief side (air cleaner side), the valve is normal if air passes into the fuel tank side but not into the check side.

Removal and Installation

Removal and installation of the various evaporative emission control system components consists of disconnecting the hoses, loosening retaining screws, and removing the part which is to be replaced or checked. Install in the reverse order. When replacing hose, make sure that it is fuel and vapor resistant.

EXHAUST EMISSION CONTROL SYSTEMS

AIR INJECTION REACTOR SYSTEM

In gasoline engines, it is difficult to burn the air/fuel mixture completely through normal combustion in the combustion chambers. Under certain operat-

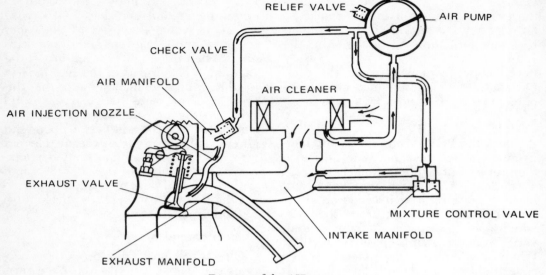

Diagram of the AIR system

ing conditions, unburned fuel is exhausted into the atmosphere.

The air injection reactor system is designed so that ambient air, pressurized by the air pump, is injected through the injection nozzles into the exhaust ports near each exhaust valve. The exhaust gases are at high temperatures and ignite when brought into contact with the oxygen of the ambient air. Thus, the unburned fuel is burned in the exhaust ports and manifold.

To act against over-rich air/fuel mixture which occurs momentarily when the throttle plates in the carburetor are rapidly closed, additional ambient air is supplied intermittently into the intake manifold through the mixture control valve.

Dual Point Distributor
(1972 and 1973)

The dual point distributor has two sets of breaker points which operate independently of each other and are positioned with a relative phase angle of 4° (1972) or 1° (1973) apart. This makes one set the advanced points and the other set the retarded points.

The two sets of points, which mechanically operate continuously, are connected in parallel to the primary side of the ignition circuit. One set of points controls the firing of the spark plugs and hence, the ignition timing, depending on whether or not the retarded set of points is energized.

When both sets of points are electrically energized, the first set to open (the advanced set, 4° or 1° sooner) has no control over breaking the ignition coil primary circuit because the retarded set is still closed and maintaining a complete circuit to ground. When the retarded set of points opens, the advanced set is still open, and the primary circuit is broken causing the electromagnetic field in the coil to collapse and the ignition spark is produced.

When the retarded set of points is removed from the primary ignition circuit through the operation of a distributor relay inserted into the retarded points circuit, the advanced set of points controls the primary circuit.

The retarded set of points is energized under the following conditions:

1. Light throttle application in Low gears: the accelerator pedal is depressed to between 7° and 35° of throttle valve opening, the clutch is engaged, and the transmission is in either 1st or 2nd gear.

2. Light throttle application or coasting in High gears: the accelerator pedal is depressed up to 35° of throttle valve opening, the clutch is engaged, and the transmission is in either 3rd or 4th gear.

In any other mode of operation, for example, with the accelerator pedal depressed less than 7° in condition No. 1,

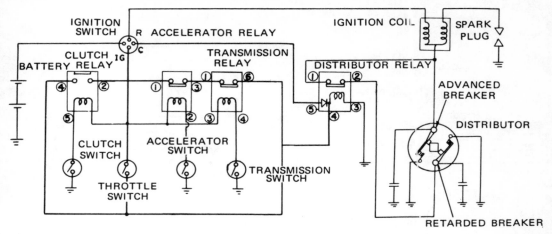

Electrical diagram of the dual point distributor system

or more than 35° in condition No. 1 or No. 2, or at anytime the clutch is disengaged, the circuit from any of the controlling switches is incomplete. This results in the distributor relay being energized which breaks the flow of current to the retarded set of points, and leaves the advance points in control of engine ignition timing.

There are four switches and relays which control the operation of the distributor relay. When the switches are On, their respective relays are energized and break an electrical circuit to the distributor relay, which in turn closes the electrical circuit to the retarded set of points, energizing them.

The switches are as follows:

1. The throttle switch: located on the carburetor primary throttle valve linkage and is turned On when the throttle valve is opened beyond 35°.

2. The transmission switch: located on the upper part of the transmission gearbox and is turned On when the transmission is shifted into 3rd or 4th gear.

3. The clutch switch: located on the clutch pedal arm and is turned On when the clutch pedal is depressed.

4. The accelerator switch: located on the accelerator pedal linkage and is turned On when the throttle valve is opened to an angle of 7°.

The purpose of the dual point distributor is to allow ignition advance only when the vehicle is accelerating heavily, or when the engine is at idle.

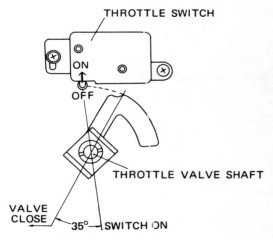

Diagram of the throttle switch

The distributor vacuum advance mechanism produces a spark advance based on the amount of vacuum in the intake manifold. With a high vacuum, less air/fuel mixture enters the engine cylinders and the mixture is therefore less highly compressed. Consequently, this mixture burns more slowly and the advance mechanism gives it more time to burn. This longer burning time results in higher combustion temperatures at peak pressure and hence, more time for nitrogen to react with oxygen and form nitrogen oxides (NO_x). At the same time, this advance timing results in less complete combustion due to the greater area of cylinder wall (quench area) exposed at the instant of ignition. This "cooled" fuel will not burn as readily and hence,

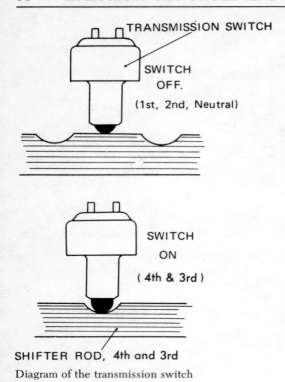

Diagram of the transmission switch

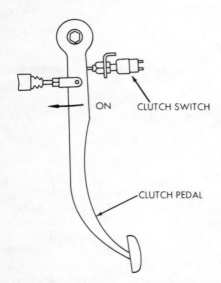

Diagram of the clutch switch (1972–73). On 1974 models the clutch switch controls only the coasting richer solenoid and is Off when depressed.

results in higher unburned hydrocarbons (HC). The production of NO_x and HC resulting from vacuum advance is highest during idle and moderate acceleration in lower gears.

Retardation of the ignition timing is necessary to reduce NO_x and HC emissions. Various ways of retarding the igni-

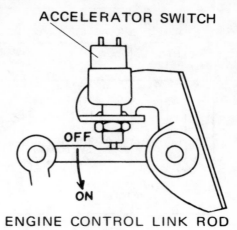

Diagram of the accelerator switch

tion spark have been used in domestic automobiles, all of which remove vacuum to the distributor vacuum advance mechanism at different times under certain conditions. Another way of accomplishing the same goal is the dual point distributor system.

NOTE: *The transmission, clutch, and accelerator switches and relays also control the operation of the Coasting Richer System.*

COASTING RICHER SYSTEM

While the engine is coasting the air/fuel mixture remains lean, preventing efficient reburning of unburned exhaust gases which can only be done with the addition of more air. Therefore, it is necessary to enrich the air/fuel mixture while the engine is coasting to attain efficient reburning of exhaust gases.

However, enriching the air/fuel mixture with only the mixture adjusting screw will cause poor engine idle, or invite an increase in the carbon monoxide (CO) content of the exhaust gases.

The coasting richer system consists of an independent operative auxiliary fuel system. This system functions when the engine is coasting, to enrich the air/fuel mixture, which minimizes hydrocarbon content of the exhaust gases through efficient combustion. This is accomplished without adversely affecting engine idle and the carbon monoxide content of the exhaust gases.

A solenoid operated valve in the carburetor allows extra fuel to be drawn into the intake manifold. The solenoid

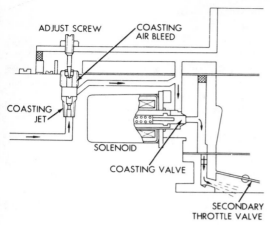

Diagram of the coasting richer system solenoid

valve is electrically connected in series to a transmission 4th/3rd gear switch, accelerator switch and a clutch switch, all of which are used to detect engine coasting conditions.

When all of these switches turn on or when the engine is coasting, the solenoid valve on the secondary side of the carburetor energizes and causes the valve to open. When the valve opens, fuel is drawn out of the float chamber by engine vacuum and metered via the coasting jet below the secondary throttle valve.

As a result of the operation of the coasting richer system, the air/fuel mixture becomes temporarily enriched to facilitate efficient reburning of exhaust gases in the exhaust manifold, thereby reducing hydrocarbon and carbon monoxide content in the exhaust gases exiting to the atmosphere.

When the engine coasting condition is halted (when the accelerator pedal is depressed, the clutch pedal depressed (1972–73 models) or when the transmission is placed in Neutral), the coasting richer circuit is opened and causes the coasting richer valve to close, shutting off the supply of extra fuel.

The solenoid switch is linked to the secondary side of the carburetor. The solenoid valve is electrically controlled by means of the accelerator switch, clutch switch, and the transmission switch.

The accelerator switch is connected to the engine accelerator linkage and is

turned Off when the throttle valve is open to an angle of 7°.

The clutch switch is installed in a position near the clutch pedal and turns Off when the clutch pedal is depressed.

The transmission switch is installed on the upper part of the transmission gearbox and turns On when the transmission is shifted into 4th or 3rd gear. The switch is Off in all other gear ranges and the coasting richer circuit is broken and the system deenergized.

EXHAUST GAS RECIRCULATION SYSTEM (EGR)

Exhaust gas recirculation is used to reduce combustion temperatures in the engine, thereby reducing the oxides of nitrogen emissions.

An EGR valve is mounted on the center of the intake manifold. The recycled exhaust gas is drawn into the bottom of the intake manifold riser portion through the exhaust manifold heat stove and EGR valve. A vacuum diaphragm is connected to a timed signal port at the carburetor flange.

As the throttle valve is opened, vacuum is applied to the EGR valve vacuum diaphragm. When the vacuum reaches about 3.5 in. Hg, the diaphragm moves against spring pressure and is in a fully up position at 8 in. Hg of vacuum. As the diaphragm moves up, it opens the exhaust gas metering valve which allows exhaust gas to be pulled into the engine intake manifold. The system does not operate when the engine is idling because the exhaust gas recirculation would cause a rough idle.

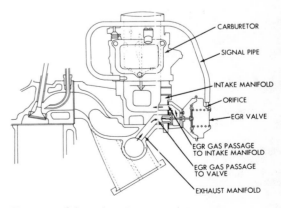

Diagram of the exhaust gas recirculation system

TEMPERATURE CONTROLLED AIR CLEANER

The rate of fuel atomization varies with the temperature of the air that the fuel is being mixed with. The air/fuel ratio cannot be held constant for efficient fuel combustion with a wide range of air temperatures. Cold air being drawn into the engine causes a denser and more richer air/fuel mixture, inefficient fuel atomization, and thus, more hydrocarbons in the exhaust gas. Hot air being drawn into the engine causes a leaner air/fuel mixture and more efficient atomization and combustion for less hydrocarbons in the exhaust gases.

The automatic temperature controlled air cleaner is designed so that the temperature of the ambient air being drawn into the engine is automatically controlled, to hold the temperature of the air and, consequently, the fuel/air ratio at a constant rate for efficient fuel combustion.

A temperature sensing vacuum switch controls vacuum applied to a vacuum motor operating a valve in the intake snorkle of the air cleaner. When the engine is cold or the air being drawn into the engine is cold, the vacuum motor opens the valve, allowing air heated by the exhaust manifold to be drawn into the engine. As the engine warms up, the temperature sensing unit shuts off the vacuum applied to the vacuum motor which allows the valve to close, shutting off the heated air and allowing cooler, outside (under hood) air to be drawn into the engine.

Inspection and Adjustments

AIR PUMP

If the air pump makes an abnormal noise and cannot be corrected without removing the pump from the vehicle, check the following in sequence:

1. Turn the pulley ¾ of a turn in the clockwise direction and ¼ of a turn in the counterclockwise direction. If the pulley is binding and if rotation is not smooth, a defective bearing is indicated.

2. Check the inner wall of the pump body, vanes and rotor for wear. If the rotor has abnormal wear, replace the air pump.

3. Check the needle roller bearing for wear and damage. If the bearings are defective, the air pump should be replaced.

4. Check and replace the rear side seal if abnormal wear or damage is noticed.

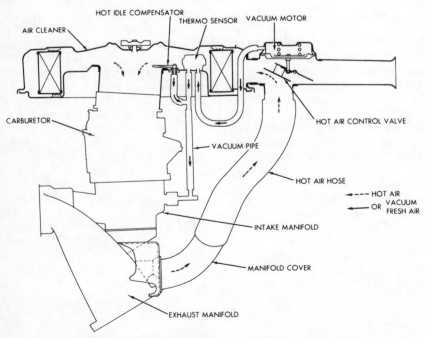

Diagram of the temperature controlled air cleaner

5. Check and replace the carbon shoes holding the vanes if they are found to be worn or damaged.

6. A deposit of carbon particles on the inner wall of the pump body and vanes is normal, but should be removed with compressed air before reassembling the air pump.

CHECK VALVE

Remove the check valve from the air manifold. Test it for leakage by blowing air into the valve from the air pump side and from the air manifold side. Air should only pass through the valve from the air pump side if the valve is functioning normally. A small amount of air leakage from the manifold side can be overlooked. Replace the check valve if it is found to be defective.

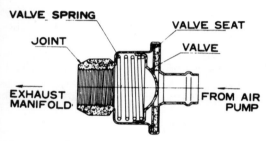

A cutaway diagram of the check valve

MIXTURE CONTROL VALVE

Disconnect the rubber hose connecting the mixture control valve with the intake manifold and plug the intake manifold side of the valve. If the mixture control valve is operating correctly, air will continue to blow out the mixture control valve for a few seconds after the accelerator pedal is fully depressed (engine running) and released quickly. If air continues to blow out for more than five seconds, replace the mixture control valve.

AIR MANIFOLD AND AIR INJECTION NOZZLES

Check around the air manifold for air leakage with the engine running at 2,000 rpm. If air is leaking from the eye joint bolt, retighten or replace the gasket. Check the air nozzles for restrictions by blowing air into the nozzles.

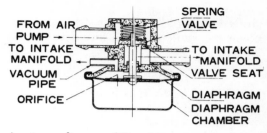

A cutaway diagram of the mixture control valve

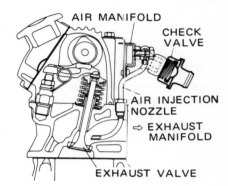

The air injection manifold and nozzles

HOSES

Check and replace hoses if they are found to be weakened or cracked. Check all hose connections and clips. Be sure that the hoses are not in contact with other parts of the engine.

COASTING RICHER SYSTEM

Operation of the coasting richer system can be checked by carefully listening for the noise associated with the operation of the solenoid valve.

Check the setting of the accelerator switch and the clutch switch. The clearance between the switch plungers and the actuating surfaces of the accelerator pedal and clutch pedal are to be 0.04–0.05 in. and 0.0197–0.0394 in. (1974 only), respectively. Test the operation of the switches with a test light connected to the electrical connectors. The switches are normally On when the pedals are released, and Off when the pedals are depressed. If the switches do not work in response to the movement of the pedals, replace the switches.

Check the operation of the transmission switch by moving the gearshift lever with the switch wiring disconnected and a test light connected to the switch terminals. The switch should only be On when the gearshift lever is shifted into either 3rd or 4th gear. Replace the switch if it is found to be defective.

EGR Valve

NOTE: *The EGR valve cannot be disassembled. No actual service is required except to determine proper operation of the valve.*

Check the valve shaft for proper movement by opening the throttle to give 2,000–2,500 rpm. The shaft should move upward at these speeds and return to the downward position when the engine speed is reduced to normal idle speed.

Check the vacuum diaphragm function by applying an outside vacuum source to the vacuum supply tube at the top of the vacuum diaphragm. The diaphragm should not leak down and should move to the fully up position at about 8–10 in. Hg of vacuum.

Fuel System

MECHANICAL FUEL PUMP

The fuel pump is a mechanically-operated, diaphragm-type driven by the fuel pump eccentric cam on the jackshaft.

Design of the fuel pump permits disassembly, cleaning and repair or replacement of defective parts.

Removal and Installation

1. Disconnect the rubber hose at the side of the fuel pump.

2. Remove the joint bolt and disconnect the fuel line at the side of the fuel pump. Be careful not to lose the joint bolt gaskets when removing the joint bolt.

3. Remove the two fuel pump mounting nuts and remove the fuel pump assembly from the side of the engine.

4. Install the fuel pump in the reverse order of removal, using a new gasket and sealer on the mating surface.

CARBURETOR

The carburetor used on the Chevy LUV is a two-barrel downdraft type with a low-speed (primary) side and a high-speed (secondary) side.

Removal and Installation

1. Remove the air cleaner wing nut and disconnect the rubber hoses from the clips on the air cleaner cover and the vacuum hose from the vacuum motor.

2. Remove the bracket bolts at the air cleaner and remove the air cleaner cover and filter element.

3. Disconnect the hot air hose (to the hot air duct), the air hose to the air pump at the air cleaner, and the vacuum hose at the joint nipple side of the intake manifold.

4. Loosen the bolt clamping the air cleaner to the carburetor. Separate the air cleaner body from the carburetor but do not remove it completely as the hoses remain connected.

5. Disconnect the PCV hose (to the camshaft cover), the rubber hoses to the check and relief valve and remove the air cleaner body.

6. On the 1974–75 models, disconnect the vacuum hoses from the EGR valve.

7. Disconnect the choke control wire.

8. Disconnect the lead from the throttle solenoid.

9. Disconnect the throttle linkage return spring.

10. Disconnect the accelerator linkage wire.

11. Disconnect the fuel line at the carburetor.

12. On 1974 and later models, remove the check valve from the air manifold.

13. Remove the four retaining nuts and lockwashers securing the carburetor to the manifold and remove the carburetor.

14. Install the carburetor in the reverse order of removal.

Throttle Linkage Adjustment

When the primary throttle valve is opened to an angle of 50° from its closed position, the adjust plate which is interlocked with the primary throttle valve, is brought into contact with portion A (see illustration) of the return plate. When the primary throttle valve is opened farther, the return plate is pulled apart from the stopper (B in the illustra-

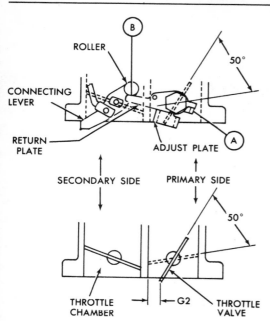

Throttle linkage adjustment

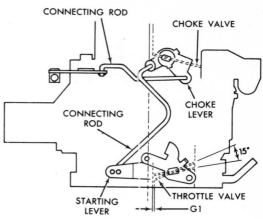

Choke and fast idle adjustment

tion), allowing the secondary throttle valve to open.

To adjust the linkage:

1. Measure the clearance between the primary throttle valve and the wall of the throttle chamber at the center of the throttle valve when the adjust plate is brought into contact with portion A of the return plate. Standard clearance is 0.26–0.32 in.

2. If necessary, make the adjustment by bending the portion A of the return plate.

Float Level Adjustment

The fuel level is normal if it is within the lines on the window glass of the float chamber when the vehicle is resting on level ground and the engine is off.

If the fuel level is outside the lines, remove the float housing cover. Have an absorbent cloth under the cover to catch the fuel from the fuel bowl. Adjust the float level by bending the needle seat on the float.

The needle valve should have an effective stroke of about 0.059 in. When necessary, the needle valve stroke can be adjusted by bending the float stopper.

NOTE: *Be careful not to bend the needle valve rod when installing the float and baffle plate, if removed.*

Choke and Fast Idle Adjustment

When the choke is pulled completely closed, the primary throttle valve is opened, by means of the choke connecting rod to an angle of 17.5°.

To check the opening angle of the primary throttle valve, close the choke valve completely and measure the clearance between the throttle valve and the wall of the throttle valve chamber at the center part of the throttle valve. The clearance should be 0.057–0.065 in. If necessary, adjust the throttle valve opening angle by bending the connecting rod. Make sure to turn the throttle stop screw all the way in before measuring the clearance.

Overhaul

Efficient carburetion depends greatly on careful cleaning and inspection during overhaul, since dirt, gum, water, or varnish in or on the carburetor parts are often responsible for poor performance.

Overhaul your carburetor in a clean, dust-free area. Carefully disassemble the carburetor, referring often to the exploded views. Keep all similar and look-alike parts segregated during disassembly and cleaning to avoid accidental interchange during assembly. Make a note of all jet sizes.

When the carburetor is disassembled, wash all parts (except diaphragms, electric choke units, pump plunger, and any other plastic, leather, fiber, or rubber parts) in clean carburetor solvent. Do not leave parts in the solvent any longer than is necessary to sufficiently loosen

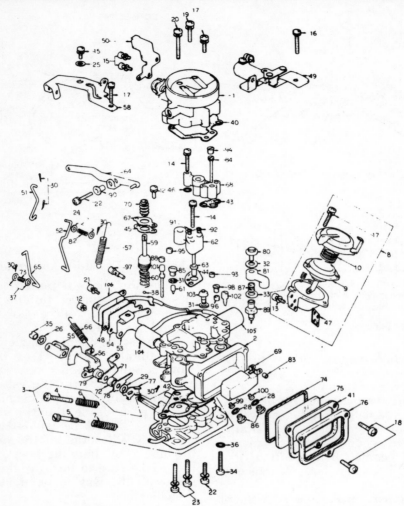

An exploded view of the carburetor used on 1972 and 1973 models

1. Choke Chamber Assy.	53. Accelerator Switch Holder	80. Set Screw
2. Float Chamber Assy.	54. Plate	81. Joint nipple
3. Throttle Chamber Assy.	55. Throttle Lever	82. Spring
4. Throttle Adjusting Screw	56. Accelerator Switch Lever	83. Float Collar
5. Idle Adjusting Screw	57. Return Spring	84. Sec. Emulsion Tube
6. Adjusting Spring Screw	58. Accelerator Switch Bracket	85. Injector Weight Plug
7. Adjusting Screw Spring	59. Accelerator Pump Piston	86. Main Jet Plug
8. Diaphragm, Chamber Assy.	60. Pump Return Spring	87. Strainer
9. Diaphragm Assy.	61. Injector Weight	88. Pri. Slow Jet Plug
10. Diaphragm Spring	62. Pri. Small Venturi	89. Float Needle Valve Assy.
12.–23. Screw	63. Outer Emulsion Tube	90. Collar
24.–26. Washer	64. Pump Lever	91. Pri. Main Air Bleed
28. Gasket	65. Pump Connecting Lever	92. Accelerator Air Bleed
29. Washer	66. Return Spring	93. Sec. Slow Air Bleed
30. Pin	67. Piston Plate	94. Sec. Main Air Bleed
31. Gasket	68. Sec. Small Venturi	95. Pri. Slow Air Bleed
32. Washer	69. Float	96. Coasting Jet
33. Gasket	70. Dust Cover	97. Vacuum Jet
34. Screw	71. Choke Connecting Lever	98. Coasting Air Bleed
35. Nut	72. Sleeve (B)	99. Pri. Main Jet
36. 37. Washer	73. Spring	100. Sec. Main Jet
38. Inlet Valve	74. Rubber Seal	101. Pri. Slow Jet
40.–48. Gasket	75. Level Gauge	102. Sec. Slow Jet
49. Choke Wire Bracket	76. Level Gauge Cover	103. Power Valve
50. Spring Hanger	77. Adjust Lever	104. Anti Dieseling Solenoid
51. Choke Connecting Rod	78. Return Plate	105. Coasting Valve Solenoid
52. Choke Connecting Rod	79. Sleeve (A)	106. Accelerator Switch

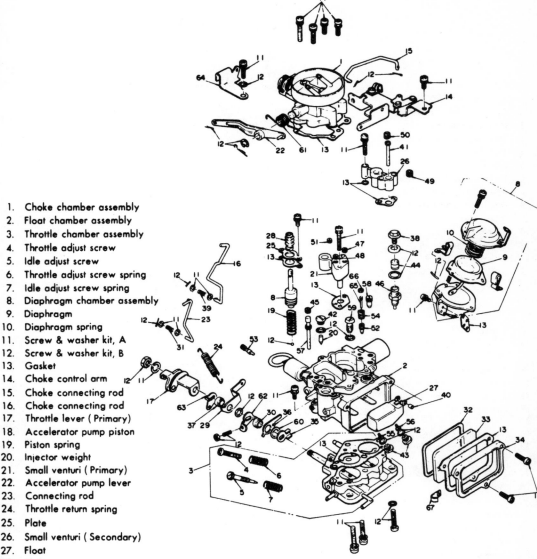

1. Choke chamber assembly
2. Float chamber assembly
3. Throttle chamber assembly
4. Throttle adjust screw
5. Idle adjust screw
6. Throttle adjust screw spring
7. Idle adjust screw spring
8. Diaphragm chamber assembly
9. Diaphragm
10. Diaphragm spring
11. Screw & washer kit, A
12. Screw & washer kit, B
13. Gasket
14. Choke control arm
15. Choke connecting rod
16. Choke connecting rod
17. Throttle lever (Primary)
18. Accelerator pump piston
19. Piston spring
20. Injector weight
21. Small venturi (Primary)
22. Accelerator pump lever
23. Connecting rod
24. Throttle return spring
25. Plate
26. Small venturi (Secondary)
27. Float
28. Dust cover
29. Starting lever
30. Sleeve
31. Spring
32. Rubber seal
33. Fuel level gage
34. Cover
35. Adjust lever, B
36. Return plate
37. Sleeve
38. Filter set screw
39. Spring
40. Collar
41. Secondary emulsion tube
42. Plug
43. Drain plug
44. Filter
45. Slow jet plug (Primary)

46. Needle valve
47. Accel air bleed
48. Main air bleed (Primary)
49. Slow air bleed (Secondary)
50. Main air bleed (Secondary)
51. Slow air bleed (Primary)
52. Coasting jet
53. Vacuum jet
54. Coasting air bleed
55. Main jet (Primary)
56. Main jet (Secondary)

57. Slow jet (Primary)
58. Slow jet (Secondary)
59. Power valve
60. Thrust washer
61. Pump lever return spring
62. Kick lever
63. Crank
64. Choke control cable hanger
65. Coasting adjust screw
66. Coasting adjust screw
67. EGR vacuum pipe clip

An exploded view of the carburetor used on 1974 and 1975 models without air conditioning

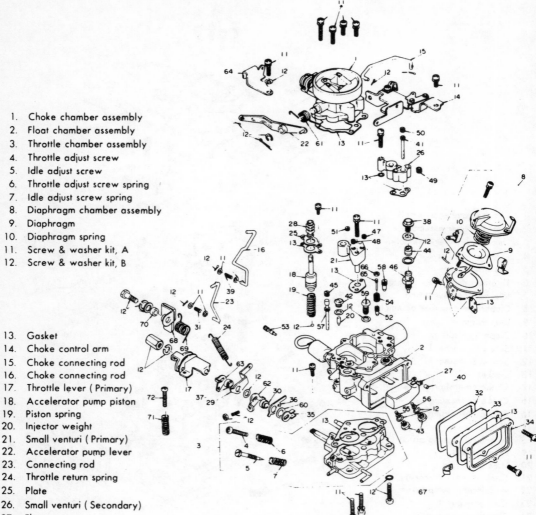

An exploded view of the carburetor used on 1974 and 1975 models with air conditioning

1. Choke chamber assembly
2. Float chamber assembly
3. Throttle chamber assembly
4. Throttle adjust screw
5. Idle adjust screw
6. Throttle adjust screw spring
7. Idle adjust screw spring
8. Diaphragm chamber assembly
9. Diaphragm
10. Diaphragm spring
11. Screw & washer kit, A
12. Screw & washer kit, B

13. Gasket
14. Choke control arm
15. Choke connecting rod
16. Choke connecting rod
17. Throttle lever (Primary)
18. Accelerator pump piston
19. Piston spring
20. Injector weight
21. Small venturi (Primary)
22. Accelerator pump lever
23. Connecting rod
24. Throttle return spring
25. Plate
26. Small venturi (Secondary)
27. Float
28. Dust cover
29. Starting lever
30. Sleeve
31. Spring
32. Rubber seal
33. Fuel level gage
34. Cover
35. Adjust lever, B
36. Return plate
37. Sleeve
38. Filter set screw
39. Spring
40. Collar
41. Secondary emulsion tube
42. Plug
43. Drain plug
44. Filter
45. Slow jet plug (Primary)
46. Needle valve
47. Accel air bleed
48. Main air bleed (Primary)

49. Slow air bleed (Secondary)
50. Main air bleed (Secondary)
51. Slow air bleed (Primary)
52. Coasting jet
53. Vacuum jet
54. Coasting air bleed
55. Main jet (Primary)
56. Main jet (Secondary)
57. Slow jet (Primary)
58. Slow jet (Secondary)
59. Power valve
60. Thrust washer

61. Pump lever return spring
62. Kick lever
63. Crank
64. Choke control cable hanger
65. Coasting adjust screw
66. Lock nut
67. EGR Vacuum pipe clip
68. Fast idle lever
69. Spring
70. Collar
71. Fast idle adjust spring
72. Fast idle adjust screw

the deposits. Excessive cleaning may remove the special finish from the float bowl and choke valve bodies, leaving these parts unfit for service. Rinse all parts in clean solvent and blow them dry with compressed air or allow them to air dry. Wipe clean all cork, plastic, leather, and fiber parts with a clean, lint-free cloth.

Blow out all passages and jets with compressed air and be sure that there are no restrictions or blockages. Never use wire or similar tools to clean jets, fuel passages, or air bleeds. Clean all jets and valves separately to avoid accidental interchange.

Check all parts for wear or damage. If wear or damage is found, replace the defective parts. Especially check the following:

1. Check the float needle and seat for wear. If wear is found, replace the complete assembly.

2. Check the float hinge pin for wear and the float(s) for dents or distortion. Replace the float if fuel has leaked into it.

3. Check the throttle and choke shaft bores for wear or an out-of-round condition. Damage or wear to the throttle arm, shaft, or shaft bore will often require replacement of the throttle body. These parts require a close tolerance of fit; wear may allow air leakage, which could affect starting and idling.

NOTE: *Throttle shafts and bushings are not included in overhaul kits. They can be purchased separately.*

4. Inspect the idle mixture adjusting needles for burrs or grooves. Any such condition requires replacement of the needle, since you will not be able to obtain a satisfactory idle.

5. Test the accelerator pump check valves. They should pass air one way but not the other. Test for proper seating by blowing and sucking on the valve. Replace the valve if necessary. If the valve is satisfactory, wash the valve again to remove breath moisture.

6. Check the bowl cover for warped surfaces with a straightedge.

7. Closely inspect the valves and seats for wear and damage, replacing as necessary.

8. After the carburetor is assembled, check the choke valve for freedom of operation.

Carburetor overhaul kits are recommended for each overhaul. These kits contain all gaskets and new parts to replace those that deteriorate most rapidly. Failure to replace all parts supplied with the kit (especially gaskets) can result in poor performance later.

Some carburetor manufacturers supply overhaul kits of three basic types: minor repair; major repair; and gasket kits. Basically, they contain the following:

Minor Repair Kits:
    All gaskets
    Float needle valve
    Volume control screw
    All diaphragms
    Spring for the pump diaphragm
Major Repair Kits:
    All jets and gaskets
    All diaphragms
    Float needle valve
    Volume control screw
    Pump ball valve
    Main jet carrier
    Float
    Complete intermediate rod
    Intermediate pump lever
    Complete injector tube
    Some cover hold-down screws and washers
Gasket Kits:
    All gaskets

Carburetor Specifications

Year	Main Jet		Idle Jet		Power Jet	Coasting Jet	Throttle Valve Angle with Choke Closed
	Primary	Secondary	Primary	Secondary			
1972	0.043 in.	0.061 in.	0.020 in.	0.032 in.	0.016 in.	0.017 in.	17°
1973	0.045 in.	0.061 in.	0.020 in.	0.032 in.	0.016 in.	0.017 in.	18.5°
1974–75	#115	#155	#50	#80	#40	#43	17.5°

After cleaning and checking all components, reassemble the carburetor, using new parts and referring to the exploded view. When reassembling, make sure that all screws and jets are tight in their seats, but do not overtighten as the tips will be distorted. Tighten all screws gradually, in rotation. Do not tighten needle valves into their seats; uneven jetting will result. Always use new gaskets. Be sure to adjust the float level when reassembling.

5 · Chassis Electrical

Heater

BLOWER

Removal and Installation

1972 ONLY

1. Disconnect the battery ground cable.

2. Drain the cooling system.

3. Disconnect the heater hoses at the heater assembly. Cap or tape the open hoses and lines to prevent coolant spillage during removal.

4. Remove the two heater control-to-instrument panel screws (use the access holes in the lower flange of the control), the lower control and disconnect the blower switch electrical leads.

5. Remove the heater case-to-dash panel screws and lower the assembly to the floor. Disconnect the resistor electrical leads and remove the defroster door and air door bowden cables at the door bellcranks. Disconnect the defroster hoses at the floor outlet and remove the assembly from the vehicle.

6. Remove the six screws attaching the floor outlet assembly to the heater case halves and then gently pry the floor outlet from the case.

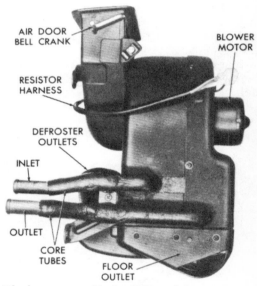

The heater assembly for 1972 models

7. Remove the front-to-rear case screws and separate the case halves.

8. Using pliers, crimp the blower motor ground wire tab in half and push it through the rear case half.

9. Remove the blower-to-rear case screws and remove the blower motor assembly.

10. Install the motor and heater as-

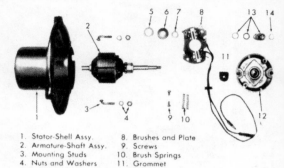

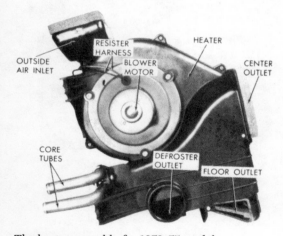

1. Stator Shell Assembly
2. Mounting Studs
3. Nuts and Lockwashers
4. Grommet
5. Armature Assembly
6. Spacers and Washers
7. Snap Ring
8. End Plate Assembly
9. Brushes and Plate
10. Screws

An exploded view of the blower motor for 1972 models

1. Stator-Shell Assy.
2. Armature-Shaft Assy.
3. Mounting Studs
4. Nuts and Washers
5. Felt Ring
6. Dust Seal
7. Spacer
8. Brushes and Plate
9. Screws
10. Brush Springs
11. Grommet
12. End Plate
13. Spacers and Washers
14. Snap Ring

An exploded view of the blower motor for 1973–75 models

sembly in the reverse order of removal and refill the cooling system.

1973 AND 1974

1. Disconnect the battery ground cable.

2. Disconnect the blower motor electrical leads.

3. Remove the blower-to-heater core screws and remove the blower motor assembly.

4. Install in the reverse order.

The heater assembly for 1973–75 models

HEATER CORE

Removal and Installation

1972

1. Remove the heater assembly as outlined under "Blower Motor Removal and Installation" for 1972, Steps 1 through 5.

2. Remove the blower motor.

3. Remove the core from the front half of the heater case.

4. Install in the reverse order of removal.

1973 AND 1974

1. Disconnect the battery ground cable.

2. Place a drain pan under the heater hoses at the heater and remove the heater hoses from the core tubes, securing the heater hoses in a raised position to prevent further loss of coolant. Plug or tape the heater core tubes to prevent spillage of coolant in the passenger compartment when removing.

3. Remove the five parcel shelf attaching screws and remove the shelf.

4. Loosen the air diverter and defroster door bowden cable clamps at the heater case and disconnect the cables from the doors.

5. Disconnect the blower resistor leads.

6. Remove the control assembly-to-instrument panel screws and swing the control to the left and lay it on the floor. Be careful not to kink the water valve bowden cable.

7. Remove the four heater-to-dash screws. Pull the heater rearward until the core tubes clear the dash opening, then remove the heater by moving it to the right and down.

8. Remove the core tube clamp screw and remove the clamp.

9. Remove the seven screws and separate the heater case halves.

10. Remove the core from the case.

11. Install and assemble the heater core and heater case in the reverse order of removal, using new seals around the heater core.

Radio

Removal and Installation

1. Disconnect the battery ground cable.

2. Remove the ash tray and ash tray plate.

3. Remove the tuner and volume control knobs, jam nuts, plain washers and face panel.

4. Remove the screws from the front and rear mounting brackets.

5. Disconnect the electrical connections, antenna lead and remove the

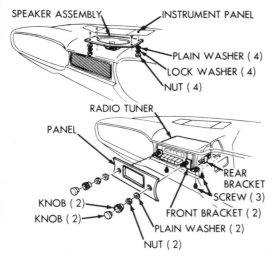

Installation of the radio

radio. Remove the front mounting brackets from the radio.

6. Install the radio in the reverse order of removal.

Windshield Wipers

MOTOR AND LINKAGE

Removal and Installation

1. Remove the wiper blades and arms.

2. Remove the two bolts attaching the pivot.

The windshield wiper motor, transmission, and linkage

3. Remove the four wiper motor mounting bolts and remove the wiper motor and linkage.

4. To remove the motor independently, take out the motor shaft nut and three bolts and then pull off the connector and disconnect the ground cable.

5. Install and assemble in the reverse order of removal. Make sure to install the wiper motor linkage so that it is not twisted or touching any adjacent parts; otherwise, the wiper motor will be loaded and cause poor wiper action.

Instrument Cluster

Removal and Installation

1. Disconnect the speedometer cable.

2. Remove the wing nuts on the rear side of the instrument panel and pull the assembly part way out.

3. Disconnect the wiring harness at the connector and remove the instrument panel.

4. Install the instrument panel in the reverse order of removal.

Removing the headlight retaining ring

Lighting

The headlight adjusting screws: A—vertical, B—horizontal

HEADLIGHTS

Removal and Installation

1. Remove the headlight trim rim.
2. Loosen the three screws attaching the sealed beam unit by turning the retaining ring counterclockwise.
3. Install the headlight by fitting the bosses on the headlight lens into the grooves so that the "TOP" mark is up.
4. Tighten the three attaching screws and install the headlight trim rim.

Wiring Diagrams

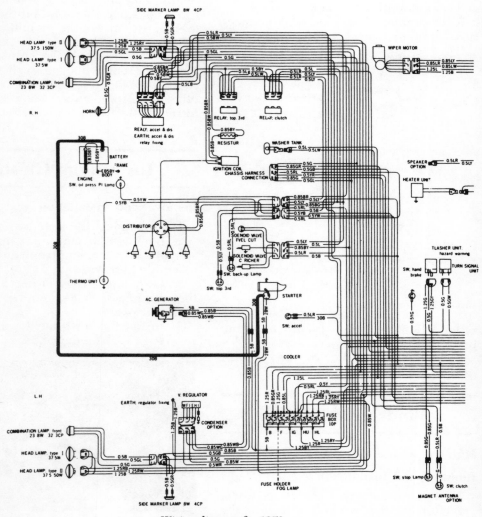

Wiring diagram for 1972

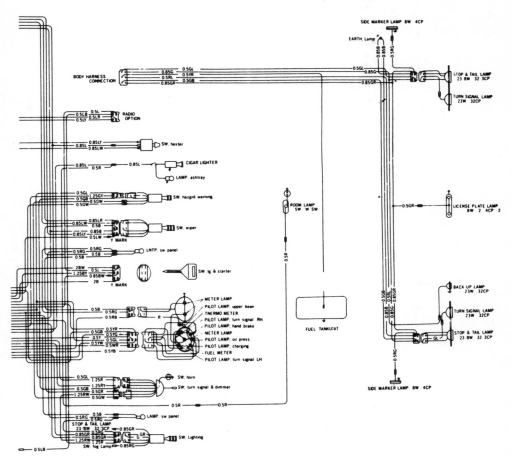

Wiring diagram for 1972

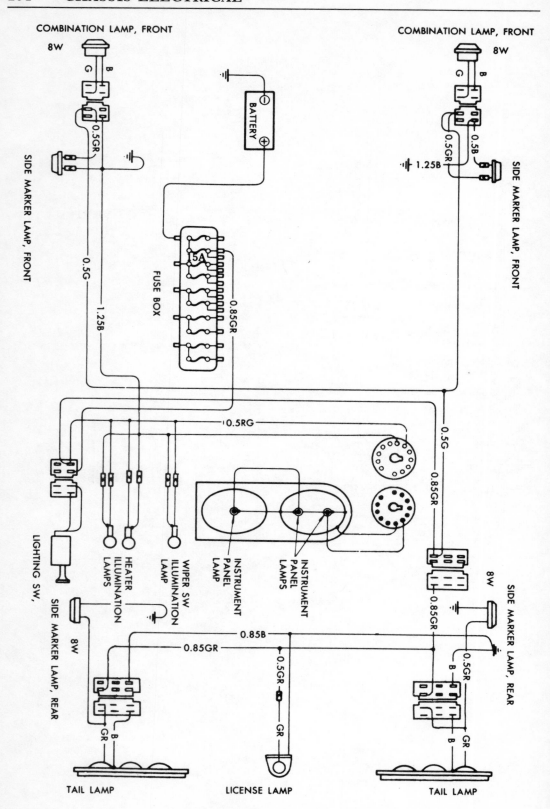

Wiring diagram for 1973

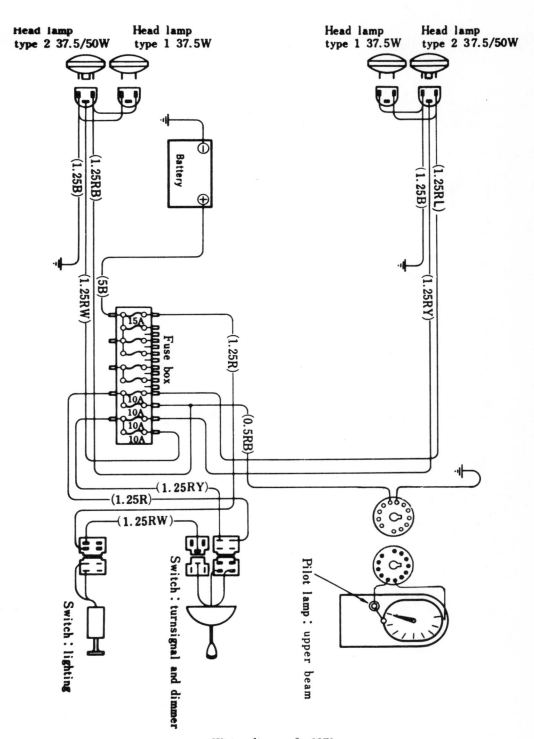

Wiring diagram for 1973

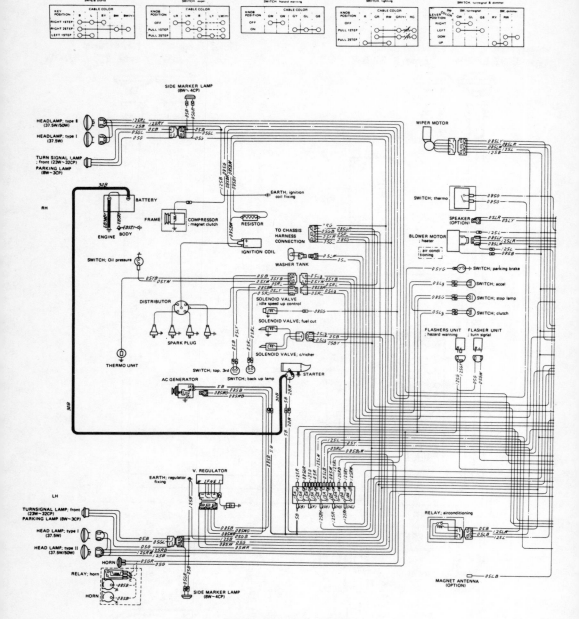

Wiring diagram for 1974

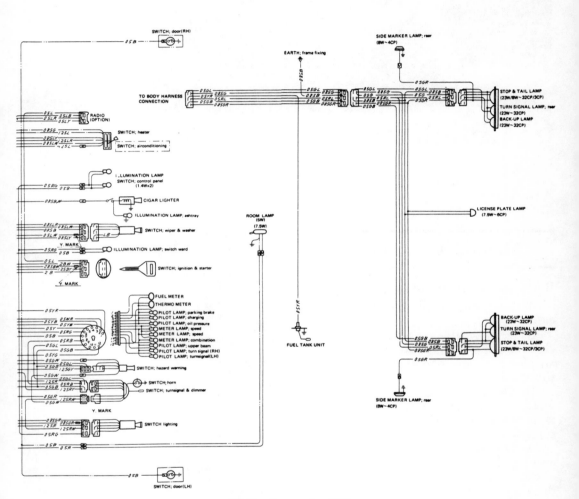

Wiring diagram for 1974

6 · Clutch and Transmission

Manual Transmission

Removal and Installation

1. Disconnect the negative battery cable.

2. Remove the air cleaner assembly, and on 1974–75 models, disconnect the accelerator linkage at the carburetor throttle lever.

3. Slide the gearshift lever boot upward on the lever, remove the two gearshift lever attaching bolts and remove the lever.

4. Remove the starter attaching bolts and lay the starter assembly aside.

5. Raise the vehicle on a hoist and disconnect the exhaust pipe at the flange and disconnect the exhaust pipe hanger at the transmission.

6. Disconnect the speedometer cable at the transmission and disconnect the driveshaft at the differential. Remove the driveshaft. At this point you will have to either drain the transmission lubricant or plug the output shaft opening to prevent spillage.

7. Disconnect the clutch slave cylinder and pushrod from the transmission case and wire the slave cylinder to the frame.

8. On the 1973–75 models, remove

Removing the gearshift lever

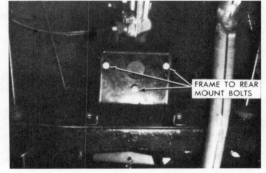

Removal of the three frame bracket-to-transmission rear mount bolts

the bolts attaching the stiffeners, then remove the stone shield (all models).

9. Remove the three frame bracket-to-rear transmission mount attaching bolts.

10. Raise the engine and transmission as required and remove the four cross-member-to-frame bracket bolts.

11. On 1973–75 models, remove the mounting from the transmission rear cover.

12. Lower the engine and transmission assembly and support the rear of the engine.

13. Disconnect the electrical connectors at the TCS switch and the back-up light switch.

14. Remove the transmission-to-engine attaching bolts and slide the transmission straight back until the input shaft is clear of the clutch. Tip the front of the transmission downward and remove the transmission from the vehicle.

15. Install the transmission in the reverse order of removal, using a clutch aligning arbor or discarded transmission input shaft to align the clutch disc and the pilot bearing, if necessary (if the clutch was removed).

Clutch

The clutch is a hydraulically operated single-plate, dry friction disc, diaphragm spring type.

The clutch is operated by a clutch pedal which is mechanically connected to a clutch master cylinder. When the pedal is depressed, the piston in the master cylinder is moved in the master cylinder bore. This movement compresses the fluid in the master cylinder causing hydraulic pressure which is transferred through a tube to the slave cylinder. The slave cylinder is mounted to the clutch housing with its piston connected to the clutch release lever. The hydraulic pressure in the slave cylinder forces the slave cylinder piston to travel out the cylinder bore and move the clutch release lever, disengaging the clutch.

Pedal Height Adjustment

1972

1. Remove the clutch pedal return spring and disconnect the clutch pedal arm from the master cylinder pushrod.

Clutch pedal height adjustment on the 1972 models

2. Loosen the clutch switch locknut at the clutch pedal bracket and adjust the height of the clutch pedal until it is flush with the brake pedal. Then retighten the locknut.

3. Adjust the pushrod end-play by rotating the clevis until $25/32$ in. of clutch pedal free-play is achieved then connect the pushrod clevis to the clutch pedal arm and tighten the through-bolt nut to 25 ft lbs and securely tighten the joint nut.

4. Install the clutch pedal return spring.

1973–75

1. Disconnect the battery ground cable.

2. Measure the clutch pedal height after making sure that the pedal is fully returned by the pedal return spring. The pedal height should be between 5.9 and 6.3 in.

3. To adjust the height, disconnect the clutch switch and remove it from its mounting bracket.

4. Loosen the locknut on the master cylinder pushrod.

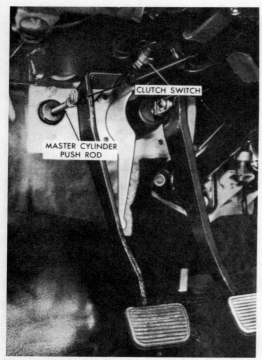

Clutch pedal height adjustment on the 1973–75 models

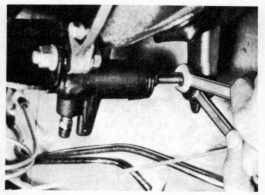

Clutch release fork adjustment

5. Adjust the clutch pedal to the specified height by rotating the pushrod in the appropriate direction. Tighten the locknut when finished with the adjustment.

6. Install the clutch switch. Adjust the clearance between the switch housing (not the switch actuating pin) and the clutch pedal tab to 0.02–0.04 in. Tighten the switch locknut.

7. Connect the electrical leads to the clutch switch and connect the negative battery cable.

Clutch Release Fork Adjustment

1. Remove the clutch release fork return spring and move the release fork slightly rearward.

2. Loosen the adjusting nut and adjust the pushrod until it contacts the release fork.

3. Back off the pushrod about 1¾ turns and tighten the locknut.

NOTE: *Excess clearance between the release (throwout) bearing and the diaphragm spring fingers will cause the clutch to drag while too little clearance can cause the clutch to slip.*

Removal and Installation

1. Raise the vehicle on a hoist.

2. Remove the transmission.

3. Mark the clutch assembly-to-flywheel relationship with paint or a center punch so that the clutch assembly can be reassembled in the same position from which it is removed.

4. Loosen the six clutch cover-to-flywheel attaching bolts, one turn at a time in an alternating sequence, until the spring tension is relieved to avoid distorting or bending the clutch cover.

5. Support the clutch pressure plate and cover assembly with a clutch aligning arbor, then remove the bolts and the clutch assembly.

6. Apply a thin coat of grease to the pressure plate wire ring, diaphragm spring, clutch cover grooves and the drive bosses on the pressure plate.

7. Apply a thin coat of Lubriplate® to the splines in the driven plate.

8. Assemble the clutch cover and pressure plate and the driven plate on a clutch alignment arbor.

9. Align the marks made on the clutch cover and the flywheel and install the six clutch cover-to-flywheel attaching bolts. Tighten the bolts to 50 in. lbs. Remove the aligning arbor.

10. Install the transmission.

CLUTCH MASTER CYLINDER

Removal and Installation

1. Disconnect the clutch pedal arm from the pushrod.

2. Disconnect the clutch hydraulic line from the master cylinder.

NOTE: *Take precautions to keep*

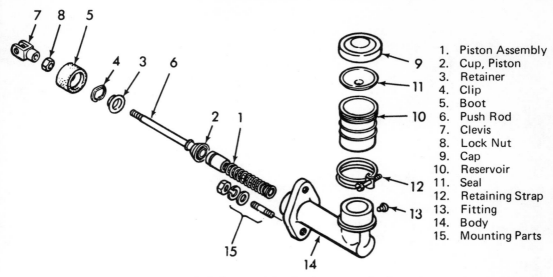

1. Piston Assembly
2. Cup, Piston
3. Retainer
4. Clip
5. Boot
6. Push Rod
7. Clevis
8. Lock Nut
9. Cap
10. Reservoir
11. Seal
12. Retaining Strap
13. Fitting
14. Body
15. Mounting Parts

An exploded view of the clutch master cylinder

brake fluid from coming in contact with any painted surfaces.

3. Remove the nuts attaching the master cylinder and remove the master cylinder and pushrod toward the engine compartment side.

4. Install the master cylinder in the reverse order of removal and bleed the clutch hydraulic system.

Overhaul

1. Remove the master cylinder from the vehicle.

2. Drain the clutch fluid from the master cylinder reservoir.

3. Remove the boot and circlip and remove the pushrod.

4. Remove the stopper, piston, cup and return spring.

5. Clean all of the parts in clean brake fluid.

6. Check the master cylinder and piston for wear, corrosion and scores and replace the parts as necessary. Light scoring and glaze can be removed with crocus cloth soaked in brake fluid.

7. Generally, the cup seal should be replaced each time the master cylinder is disassembled. Check the cup and replace it if it is worn, fatigued, or damaged.

8. Check the clutch fluid reservoir, filler cap, dust cover and the pipe for distortion and damage and replace the parts as necessary.

9. Lubricate all new parts with clean brake fluid.

10. Reassemble the master cylinder parts in the reverse order of disassembly, taking note of the following:

   a. Reinstall the cup seal carefully to prevent damaging the lipped portions;

   b. Adjust the height of the clutch pedal after installing the master cylinder in position on the vehicle;

   c. Fill the master cylinder and clutch fluid reservoir and then bleed the clutch hydraulic system.

CLUTCH SLAVE CYLINDER

Removal and Installation

1. Remove the slave cylinder attaching bolts and the pushrod from the shift fork.

2. Disconnect the flexible fluid hose from the slave cylinder and remove the unit from the vehicle.

3. Install the slave cylinder in the reverse order of removal and bleed the clutch hydraulic system.

Overhaul

1. Remove the slave cylinder from the vehicle.

2. Remove the pushrod and boot.

3. Force out the piston by blowing compressed air into the slave cylinder at the hose connection.

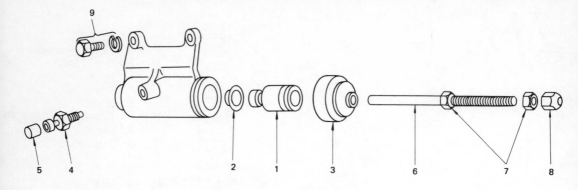

1. PISTON   4. BLEEDER SCREW   7. NUT
2. PISTON CUP   5. CAP   8. NUT
3. BOOT   6. PUSH ROD   9. BOLT

An exploded view of the clutch slave cylinder

NOTE: *Be careful not to apply excess air pressure to avoid possible injury.*

4. Clean all of the parts in clean brake fluid.

5. Check and replace the slave cylinder bore and piston if wear or severe scoring exists. Light scoring and glaze can be removed with crocus cloth soaked in brake fluid.

6. Normally the piston cup should be replaced when the slave cylinder is disassembled. Check the piston cup and replace it if it is found to be worn, fatigued or scored.

7. Replace the rubber boot if it is cracked or broken.

8. Lubricate all of the new parts in clean brake fluid and reassemble in the reverse order of disassembly, taking note of the following:

   a. Use care when reassembling the piston cup to prevent damaging the lipped portion of the piston cup;

   b. Fill the master cylinder with brake fluid and bleed the clutch hydraulic system;

   c. Adjust the clearance between the pushrod and the shift fork to 5/64 in.

BLEEDING THE CLUTCH HYDRAULIC SYSTEM

1. Check and fill the clutch fluid reservoir to the specified level as necessary. During the bleeding process, continue to check and replenish the reservoir to prevent the fluid level from getting lower than ½ the specified level.

2. Bleed the clutch master cylinder first, if it is known to have air in it.

NOTE: *Take precautionary measures to prevent the brake fluid from getting on any painted surfaces.*

3. Pump the clutch pedal several times, hold it down and loosen the bleeder screw slowly.

4. Tighten the bleeder screw and release the clutch pedal gradually. Repeat this operation until air bubbles disappear from the brake fluid being expelled out through the bleeder screw.

5. Remove the dust cap from the bleeder screw on the clutch slave cylinder and connect a tube to the bleeder screw and insert the other end of the

Bleeding the clutch hydraulic system at the slave cylinder

tube into a clean glass or metal container.

6. Repeat the bleeding procedures outlined for the master cylinder in Steps 3 and 4 until all evidence of air bubbles completely disappears from the brake fluid being pumped out through the tube.

7. When the air is completely removed, securely tighten the bleeder screw and replace the dust cap.

8. Check and refill the master cylinder reservoir as necessary.

9. Depress the clutch pedal several times to check the operation of the clutch and check for leaks.

7 · Drive Train

Driveline

DRIVESHAFT AND U-JOINTS

Removal and Installation

1. Remove the bolts connecting the flange yoke with the pinion flange and disconnect the driveshaft at the flange.
2. Pull the driveshaft assembly out from the transmission rear cover.
3. Plug or cover the end of the transmission to avoid lubricant loss.
4. Install the driveshaft in the reverse order of removal.

U-Joint Overhaul

1. Remove the driveshaft from the vehicle.
2. Punch mating marks on both the yokes at either end of the driveshaft and the driveshaft itself so that the driveshaft assembly can be reassembled in the same position.
3. Remove the snap-rings from the bearing hole of the yokes.
4. Place the yoke in a vise with a small socket positioned against one of the bearing cups and a larger socket placed against the yoke on the opposite side. The larger socket must be able to receive the bearing cap when it is pressed out of the yoke.

5. Tighten the vise until the bearing caps are free of the yoke.
6. Remove the two remaining bearings from the opposite yoke in the same manner and remove the spider bearing journal.
7. Make sure that the new spiders and needle bearings in the bearing caps are well lubricated.
8. Assemble the universal joint spider and bearing caps to the yoke in the reverse manner of removal, using the smaller socket to press the bearing caps into the yoke and the larger socket to bear against the yoke bearing cap hole at the opposite end. Use a vise to press the bearing caps in place.
9. Install the hole snap-ring to secure the bearing caps.
10. Assemble the slide yoke to the driveshaft, aligning the marks made prior to disassembly.
11. Install the driveshaft assembly on the vehicle.

Rear Axle

AXLE SHAFT

Removal and Installation

1. Raise the vehicle on a hoist.
2. Remove the rear wheel cover and the wheel and tire.

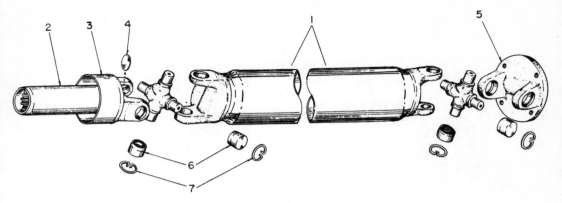

Exploded view of the driveshaft

1. Driveshaft   5. Flange yoke
2. Spline yoke   6. Bearing caps
3. Cover   7. Snap-rings
4. Plate plug

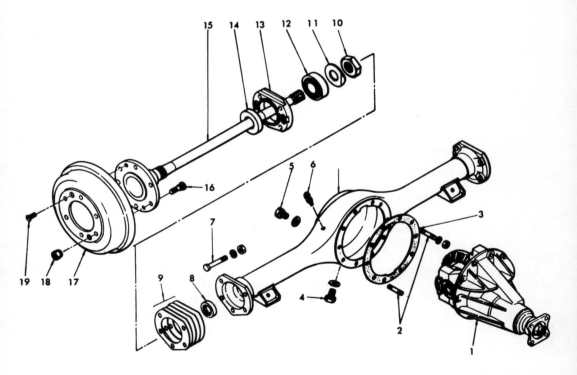

Exploded view of the axle shaft and housing assembly

1. Differential carrier   7. Through-bolt   14. Grease seal
   and case assembly   8. Oil seal   15. Axle shaft
2. Mounting bolt   9. Shims   16. Wheel stud
3. Gasket   10. Locknut   17. Brake drum
4. Drain plug   11. Lockwasher   18. Wheel nut
5. Filler plug   12. Axle shaft bearing 19. Drum-to-flange screw
6. Vent   13. Bearing holder

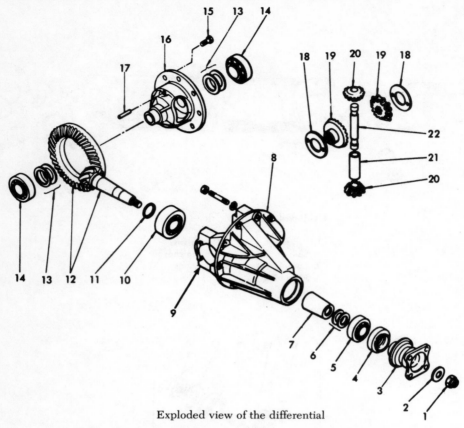

Exploded view of the differential

1. Pinion nut	9. Bearing cap	16. Differential case
2. Washer	10. Inner bearing	17. Pinion shaft lock-pin
3. Companion flange	11. Depth shim	18. Thrust washer
4. Oil seal	12. Ring and pinion	19. Differential gear
5. Outer bearing	13. Side bearing shims	20. Pinion gear
6. Preload shims	14. Side bearing	21. Thrust block
7. Spacer	15. Ring gear-to-case bolt	22. Pinion shaft
8. Differential carrier		

3. Remove the brake drum, brake shoes and disconnect the parking brake inner cable.

4. Disconnect the brake line at the wheel cylinder and plug the end of the line.

5. Remove the four nuts from the bearing holder through-bolts from the inside of the brake backing plate.

6. Using an axle puller, pull out the axle shaft assembly. Never strike the brake backing plate with a hammer in an attempt to remove the axle shaft.

7. Install the axle shaft in the reverse order of removal, tightening the bearing holding plate attaching nuts to 55 ft lbs, bleeding the brake hydraulic system after installing the brakes and adjusting the parking brake cable as necessary.

Differential

NOTE: *Differential service is best left to those extremely familiar with their vagaries and idiosyncrasies. A great many specialized tools are required as well as a good deal of experience.*

INTRODUCTION

The rear axle must transmit power through a 90° bend. To accomplish this, straight cut bevel gears or spiral bevel gears are used. This type of gear is satisfactory for differential side gears, but since the centerline of the gears must intersect, they rapidly became unsuited for ring and pinion gears. The lowering of

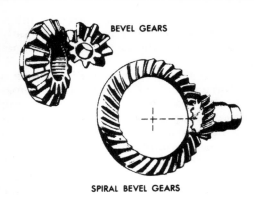

BEVEL GEARS

SPIRAL BEVEL GEARS

Bevel gears

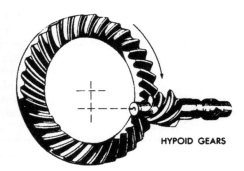

HYPOID GEARS

Hypoid gears

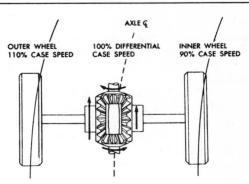

AXLE ₵

OUTER WHEEL 110% CASE SPEED

100% DIFFERENTIAL CASE SPEED

INNER WHEEL 90% CASE SPEED

Differential action during cornering

the driveshaft brought about a variation of bevel gears called the hypoid gear. This type of gear does not require a meeting of the gear centerlines and can therefore be underslung, relative to the centerline of the ring gear.

OPERATION

The differential is an arrangement of gears which permits the rear wheels to turn at different speeds when cornering and divides the torque between the axle shafts. The differential gears are mounted on a pinion shaft and the gears are free to rotate on this shaft. The pinion shaft is fitted in a bore in the differential case and is at right angles to the axle shafts.

Power flow through the differential is as follows. The drive pinion, which is turned by the driveshaft, turns the ring gear. The ring gear, which is bolted to the differential case, rotates the case. The differential pinion forces the pinion gears against the side gears. In cases where both wheels have equal traction, the pinion gears do not rotate on the pinion shaft, because the input force of the

pinion gear is divided equally between the two side gears. Consequently the pinion gears revolve with the pinion shaft, although they do not revolve on the pinion shaft itself. The side gears, which are splined to the axle shafts, and meshed with the pinion gears, rotate the axle shafts.

When it becomes necessary to turn a corner, the differential becomes effective and allows the axle shafts to rotate at different speeds. As the inner wheel slows down, the side gear splined to the inner wheel axle shaft also slows down. The pinion gears act as balancing levers by maintaining equal tooth loads to both gears while allowing unequal speeds of rotation at the axle shafts. If the vehicle speed remains constant, and the inner wheel slows down to 90 percent of vehicle speed, the outer wheel will speed up to 110 percent.

Limited-Slip Differential Operation

Limited-slip differentials provide driving force to the wheel with the best traction before the other wheel begins to spin. This is accomplished through clutch plates or cones. The clutch plates or cones are located between the side gears and inner wall of the differential case. When they are squeezed together through spring tension and outward force from the side gears, three reactions occur. Resistance on the side gears causes more torque to be exerted on the clutch packs or clutch cones. Rapid one-wheel spin cannot occur, because the side gear is forced to turn at the same speed as the case. Most important, with the side gear and the differential case turning at the same speed, the other wheel is forced to rotate in the same direction and at the same speed as the differential case. Thus driving force is applied to the wheel with the better traction.

NOTE: *Whenever the rear of a vehicle with a limited-slip rear axle is jacked or supported, both wheels must be raised off the ground. Movement of either wheel in contact with the ground can cause the vehicle to move.*

Determining Gear Ratio

Normally, the gear ratio of an axle installed in a vehicle is listed somewhere; in service manuals, on an option list, or on a tag on the axle somewhere.

Determining the axle ratio of any given axle is an esoteric subject, relatively useless until you have to know. But, as a "junkyard art" it is invaluable.

The rear axle ratio is said to have a certain ratio, say, 4.11. It is called a 4.11 rear although the 4.11 actually means 4.11:1. This means that the driveshaft will turn 4.11 times for every turn of the rear wheel. The number 4.11 is determined by dividing the number of teeth on the pinion gear into the number of teeth on the ring gear. In the case of a 4.11, there are 9 teeth on the pinion and 37 teeth on the ring gear ($37 \div 9 = 4.11$). This provides a sure way (although troublesome—except to those who are really interested) of determining your rear axle ratio. You must drain the rear axle and remove the rear cover, if it has one, and count the teeth on the ring and pinion.

An easier method is to jack and support the vehicle so that BOTH rear wheels are off the ground. Make a chalk mark on the rear wheel and the driveshaft. Block the front wheels, set the parking brake and put the transmission in Neutral. Turn the rear wheel one complete revolution and count the number of turns that the driveshaft makes. The number of turns that the driveshaft makes in one complete revolution of the rear wheel is an *approximation* of the rear axle ratio.

Differential Diagnosis

The most essential part of rear axle service is proper diagnosis of the problem. Bent or broken axle shafts or broken gears pose little problem, but isolating an axle noise and correctly interpreting the problem can be extremely difficult, even for an experienced mechanic.

Any gear driven unit will produce a certain amount of noise, therefore, a specific diagnosis for each individual unit is the best practice. Acceptable or normal noise can be classified as a slight noise heard only at certain speeds or under unusual conditions. This noise tends to reach a peak at 40–60 mph, depending on the road condition, load, gear ratio and tire size. Frequently, other noises are mistakenly diagnosed as coming from the rear axle. Vehicle noises from tires, transmission, driveshaft, U-joints and front and rear wheel bearings will often be mistaken as emanating from the rear axle. Raising the tire pressure to eliminate tire noise (although this will not silence mud or snow treads), listening for noise at varying speeds and road conditions and listening for noise at drive and coast conditions will aid in diagnosing alleged rear axle noises.

EXTERNAL NOISE ELIMINATION

It is advisable to make a thorough road test to determine whether the noise originates in the rear axle or whether it originates from the tires, engine, transmission, wheel bearings or road surface. Noise originating from other places cannot be corrected by overhauling the rear axle.

ROAD NOISE

Brick roads or rough surfaced concrete, may cause a noise which can be mistaken as coming from the rear axle. Driving on a different type of road, (smooth asphalt or dirt) will determine whether the road is the cause of the noise. Road noise is usually the same on drive or coast conditions.

TIRE NOISE

Tire noise can be mistaken as rear axle noises, even though the tires on the front are at fault. Snow tread and mud tread tires or tires worn unevenly will frequently cause vibrations which seem to originate elsewhere; *temporarily, and for test purposes only,* inflate the tires to 40–50 lbs. This will significantly alter the noise produced by the tires, but will not alter noise from the rear axle. Noises from the rear axle will normally cease at speeds below 30 mph on coast, while tire noise will continue at lower tone as car speed is decreased. The rear axle noise will usually change from drive conditions to coast conditions, while tire noise will not. Do not forget to lower the tire pressure to normal after the test is complete.

Engine and Transmission Noise

Engine and transmission noises also seem to originate in the rear axle. Road test the vehicle and determine at which speeds the noise is most pronounced. Stop the car in a quiet place to avoid interfering noises. With the transmission in Neutral, run the engine slowly through the engine speeds corresponding to the car speed at which the noise was most noticeable. If a similar noise was produced with the car standing still, the noise is not in the rear axle, but somewhere in the engine or transmission.

Front Wheel Bearing Noise

Front wheel bearing noises, sometimes confused with rear axle noises, will not change when comparing drive and coast conditions. While holding the car speed steady, lightly apply the footbrake. This will often cause wheel bearing noise to lessen, as some of the weight is taken off the bearing. Front wheel bearings are easily checked by jacking up the wheels and spinning the wheels. Shaking the wheels will also determine if the wheel bearings are excessively loose.

Rear Axle Noises

If a logical test of the vehicle shows that the noise is not caused by external items, it can be assumed that the noise originates from the rear axle. The rear axle should be tested on a smooth level road to avoid road noise. It is not advisable to test the axle by jacking up the rear wheels and running the car.

True rear axle noises generally fall into two classes: gear noise and bearing noises, and can be caused by faulty driveshaft, faulty wheel bearings, worn differential or pinion shaft bearings, U-joint misalignment, worn differential side gears and pinions, or mismatched, improperly adjusted, or scored ring and pinion gears.

Rear Wheel Bearing Noise

A rough rear wheel bearing causes a vibration or growl which will continue with the car coasting or in Neutral. A brinelled rear wheel bearing will also cause a knock or click approximately every two revolutions of the rear wheel, due to the fact that the bearing rollers do not travel at the same speed as the rear wheel and axle. Jack up the rear wheels and spin the wheel slowly, listening for signs of a rough or brinelled wheel bearing.

Differential Side Gear and Pinion Noise

Differential side gears and pinions seldom cause noise, since their movement is relatively slight on straight ahead driving. Noise produced by these gears will be more noticeable on turns.

Pinion Bearing Noise

Pinion bearing failures can be distinguished by their speed of rotation, which is higher than side bearings or axle bearings. Rough or brinelled pinion bearings cause a continuous low pitch whirring or scraping noise beginning at low speeds.

Side Bearing Noise

Side bearings produce a constant rough noise, which is slower than the pinion bearing noise. Side bearing noise may also fluctuate in the above rear wheel bearing test.

Gear Noise

Two basic types of gear noise exist. First, is the type produced by bent or broken gear teeth which have been forcibly damaged. The noise from this type of damage is audible over the entire speed range. Scoring or damage to the hypoid gear teeth generally results from insufficient lubricant, improper lubricant, improper break-in, insufficient gear backlash, improper ring and pinion gear alignment or loss of torque on the drive

Two types of damage which cause gear noise

pinion nut. If not corrected, the scoring will lead to eventual erosion or fracture of the gear teeth. Hypoid gear tooth fracture can also be caused by extended overloading of the gear set (fatigue fracture) or by shock overloading (sudden failure). Differential and side gears rarely give trouble, but common causes of differential failure are shock loading, extended overloading and differential pinion seizure at the cross-shaft, result-

ing from excessive wheel spin and consequent lubricant breakdown.

The second type of gear noise pertains to the mesh pattern between the ring and pinion gears. This type of abnormal gear noise can be recognized as a cycling pitch or whine audible in either drive, float or coast conditions. Gear noises can be recognized as they tend to peak out in a narrow speed range and remain constant in pitch, whereas bearing noises tend to vary in pitch with vehicle speeds. Noises produced by the ring and pinion gears will generally follow the pattern below.

A. Drive Noise: Produced under vehicle acceleration.

B. Coast Noise: Produced while the car coasts with a closed throttle.

C. Float Noise: Occurs while maintaining constant car speed (just enough to keep speed constant) on a level road.

D. Drive, Coast and Float Noise: These noises will vary in tone with speed and be very rough or irregular if the differential or pinion shaft bearings are worn.

GENERAL DRIVE AXLE DIAGNOSTIC GUIDE

(Also see following text for further differential diagnosis.)

CONDITION	POSSIBLE CAUSE	CORRECTION
REAR WHEEL NOISE	(a) Loose Wheel.	(a) Tighten loose wheel nuts.
	(b) Spalled wheel bearing cup or cone.	(b) Check rear wheel bearings. If spalled or worn, replace.
	(c) Defective or brinelled wheel bearing.	(c) Defective or brinelled bearings must be replaced. Check rear axle shaft end-play.
	(d) Excessive axle shaft end-play.	(d) Readjust axle shaft end play.
	(e) Bent or sprung axle shaft flange.	(e) Replace bent or sprung axle shaft.
SCORING OF DIFFERENTIAL GEARS AND PINIONS	(a) Insufficient lubrication.	(a) Replace scored gears. Scoring marks on the pressure face of gear teeth or in the bore are caused by instantaneous fusing of the mating surfaces. Scored gears should be replaced. Fill rear axle to required capacity with proper lubricant.
	(b) Improper grade of lubricant.	(b) Replace scored gears. Inspect all gears and bearings for possible damage. Clean and refill axle to required capacity with proper lubricant.
	(c) Excessive spinning of one wheel.	(c) Replace scored gears. Inspect all gears, pinion bores and shaft for scoring, or bearings for possible damage.
TOOTH BREAKAGE (RING GEAR AND PINION)	(a) Overloading.	(a) Replace gears. Examine other gears and bearings for possible damage. Avoid future overloading.
	(b) Erratic clutch operation.	(b) Replace gears, and examine remaining parts for possible damage. Avoid erratic clutch operation.
	(c) Ice-spotted pavements.	(c) Replace gears. Examine remaining parts for possible damage. Replace parts as required.
	(d) Improper adjustment.	(d) Replace gears. Examine other parts for possible damage. Be sure ring gear and pinion backlash is correct.
REAR AXLE NOISE	(a) Insufficient lubricant.	(a) Refill rear axle with correct amount of the proper lubricant. Also check for leaks and correct as necessary.
	(b) Improper ring gear and pinion adjustment.	(b) Check ring gear and pinion tooth contact.
	(c) Unmatched ring gear and pinion.	(c) Remove unmatched ring gear and pinion. Replace with a new matched gear and pinion set.
	(d) Worn teeth on ring gear or pinion.	(d) Check teeth on ring gear and pinion for contact. If necessary, replace with new matched set.
	(e) End-play in drive pinion bearings.	(e) Adjust drive pinion bearing preload.
	(f) Side play in differential bearings.	(f) Adjust differential bearing preload.
	(g) Incorrect drive gearlash.	(g) Correct drive gear lash.
	(h) Limited-Slip differential — moan and chatter.	(h) Drain and flush lubricant. Refill with proper lubricant.

CONDITION	POSSIBLE CAUSE	CORRECTION
Loss of Lubricant	(a) Lubricant level too high.	(a) Drain excess lubricant.
	(b) Worn axle shaft oil seals.	(b) Replace worn oil seals with new ones. Prepare new seals before replacement.
	(c) Cracked rear axle housing.	(c) Repair or replace housing as required.
	(d) Worn drive pinion oil seal.	(d) Replace worn drive pinion oil seal with a new one.
	(e) Scored and worn companion flange.	(e) Replace worn or scored companion flange and oil seal.
	(f) Clogged vent.	(f) Remove obstructions.
	(g) Loose carrier housing bolts or housing cover screws.	(g) Tighten bolts or cover screws to specifications and fill to correct level with proper lubricant.
Overheating of Unit	(a) Lubricant level too low.	(a) Refill rear axle.
	(b) Incorrect grade of lubricant.	(b) Drain, flush and refill rear axle with correct amount of the proper lubricant.
	(c) Bearings adjusted too tightly.	(c) Readjust bearings.
	(d) Excessive wear in gears.	(d) Check gears for excessive wear or scoring. Replace as necessary.
	(e) Insufficient ring gear-to-pinion clearance.	(e) Readjust ring gear and pinion backlash and check gears for possible scoring.

NOISE DIAGNOSIS CHART

PROBLEM	CAUSE
1. Identical noise in Drive or Coast conditions	1. Road noise Tire noise Front wheel bearing noise
2. Noise changes on a different type of road	2. Road noise Tire noise
3. Noise tone lowers as car speed is lowered	3. Tire noise
4. Similar noise is produced with car standing and driving	4. Engine noise Transmission noise
5. Vibration	5. Rough rear wheel bearing Unbalanced or damaged driveshaft Unbalanced tire Worn universal joint in driveshaft Misaligned drive shaft at companion flange Excessive companion flange runout
6. A knock or click approximately every two revolutions of rear wheel	6. Brinelled rear wheel bearing
7. Noise most pronounced on turns	7. Differential side gear and pinion wear or damage
8. A continuous low pitch whirring or scraping noise starting at relatively low speed	8. Damaged or worn pinion bearing
9. Drive noise, coast noise or float noise	9. Damaged or worn ring and pinion gear
10. Clunk on acceleration or deceleration	10. Worn differential cross-shaft in case
11. Clunk on stops	11. Insufficient grease in driveshaft slip yoke
12. Groan in Forward or Reverse	12. Improper differential lubricant
13. Chatter on turns	13. Improper differential lubricant Worn clutch plates
14. Clunk or knock during operation on rough roads.	14. Excessive end-play of axle shafts to differential cross-shaft

8 · Suspension and Steering

Front Suspension

LUV trucks are equipped with the short and long arm type front suspension. The control arms are attached to the vehicle with bolts and bushings at their inner pivot points and to the steering knuckle, which is part of the front wheel spindle, at their outer points.

The front suspension is an independent type utilizing torsion bar springs. The torsion bar has splines on each end. Height control is provided on the third crossmember of the frame. Both upper and lower control arms are pressed steel and the torsion bar is supported at the ends by forged links. The links are bolted to the third frame crossmember in the rear and the lower control arms in front.

Fore and aft movement of the front suspension is controlled by strut bars bolted to the lower control arms at one end and mounted to the chassis frame, using a rubber bumper at the other end. A torsion bar type stabilizer is connected to the lower control arm by shackle rods.

TORSION BARS

Removal and Installation

1. Jack up the front of the vehicle and support it with jackstands.
2. Remove the adjusting bolt from the height control arm.
3. Mark the location and remove the height control arm from the torsion bar and the third crossmember.

The vehicle ride height adjustment end of the torsion bar

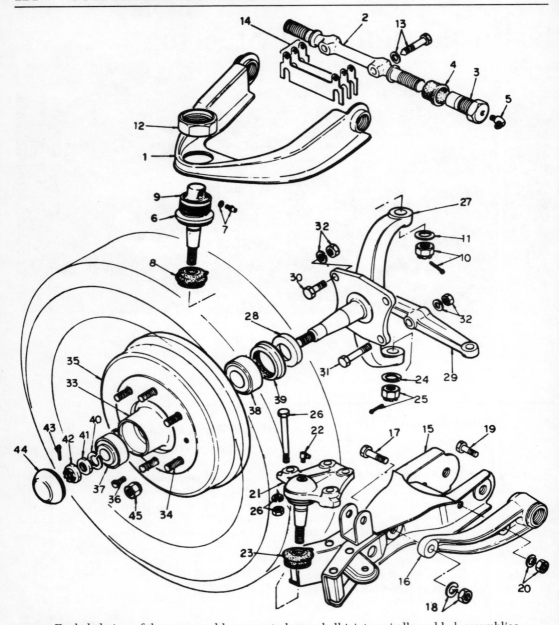

Exploded view of the upper and lower control arms, ball joints, spindle and hub assemblies

1. Upper Control Arm	16. Lower Control Arm Link	31. Bolt
2. Pivot Shaft	17. Bolt	32. Nut, Lock Washer
3. Bushing(2)	18. Nut, Lock Washer	33. Hub
4. Cover	19. Bolt	34. Wheel Stud
5. Grease Fitting	20. Nut, Lock Washer	35. Drum
6. Upper Ball Joint	21. Lower Ball Joint	36. Screw
7. Grease Fitting	22. Grease Fitting	37. Outer Wheel Bearing
8. Boot	23. Boot	38. Inner Wheel Bearing
9. Shim	24. Lock Washer	39. Grease Seal
10. Nut, Cotter Pin	25. Nut, Cotter Pin	40. Washer
11. Washer	26. Bolt, Nut, Lock Washer	41. Nut
12. Staked Nut	27. Knuckle	42. Nut Retainer
13. Bolt, Washer	28. Bearing Shoulder Piece	43. Cotter Pin
14. Shims	29. Tie Rod Link	44. Dust Cap
15. Lower Control Arm	30. Bolt	45. Wheel Stud Nut

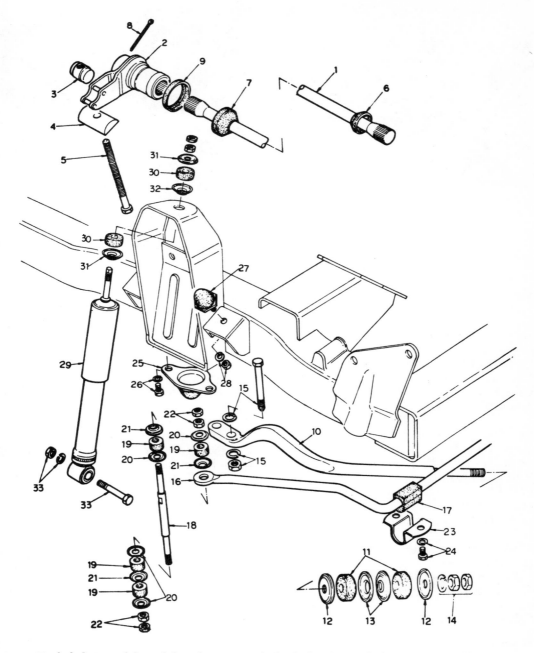

Exploded view of the stabilizer bar, strut rod, shock absorber, and torsion bar assemblies

1. Torsion Bar
2. Height Control Arm
3. Pivot Nut
4. Height Control Seat
5. Height Control Bolt
6. Boot
7. Boot
8. Cotter Pin
9. Seal
10. Strut Rod Assy.
11. Strut Rod Bushings

12. Strut Rod Washer
13. Strut Rod Washer
14. Nut, Lock Washer
15. Bolt, Washer, Nut
16. Stabilizer Bar
17. Stabilizer Bushings
18. Link Stud
19. Link Stud Bushings
20. Stabilizer Link Stud Washers
21. Stabilizer Link Stud Washers
22. Nuts

23. Stabilizer Bar Bracket
24. Bolt and Washer
25. Lower Control Arm Bumper
26. Bolt, Washer
27. Upper Control Arm Bumpers(2)
28. Nut, Washer
29. Shock Absorber
30. Bushing
31. Retainer
32. Retainer
33. Bolt, Lock Washer, Nut

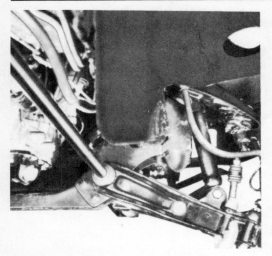

The lower control arm end of the torsion bar

Installation of the front shock absorber

4. Mark the location and withdraw the torsion bar from the lower control arm.

5. For installation, apply a generous amount of grease to the serrated ends of the torsion bars.

6. Hold the rubber bumpers in contact with the lower control arm. Jack the vehicle up under the lower control arm to accomplish this.

7. Insert the front end of the torsion bar into the control arm.

8. Install the height control arm in position so that its end is reaching the adjusting bolt. Be sure to lubricate the part of the height control arm that fits into the chassis with grease.

9. Install a new cotter pin in the control arm.

10. Turn the adjusting bolt to the location marked before removal.

11. Lower the vehicle and check the vehicle height and trim attitude.

SHOCK ABSORBERS

Removal and Installation

1. Raise the vehicle and support it with jackstands.

2. Hold the upper stem of the shock absorber from turning with an open-end wrench, and then, remove the upper stem retaining nut, retainer and rubber grommet.

3. Remove the bolt retaining the lower shock absorber pivot to the lower control arm and remove the shock absorber from the vehicle.

4. Install the shock absorber by first installing the lower retainer and rubber grommet over the upper stem and then, installing the shock fully extended up through the upper control arm so that the upper stem passes through the mounting hole in the frame bracket.

5. Install the upper rubber grommet, retainer and attaching nut over the shock absorber upper stem.

6. Hold the upper stem of the shock absorber from turning with an open-end wrench and tighten the retaining nut.

7. Install the retainers attaching the shock absorber lower pivot to the lower control arm and tighten them.

8. Lower the vehicle.

UPPER CONTROL ARM AND BALL JOINT

Removal and Installation

NOTE: *The upper control arm and ball joint are replaced as an assembly.*

1. Raise the vehicle and support it on jackstands placed under the lower control arms.

2. Remove the wheel and tire assembly.

3. Remove the cotter pin nut fastening the upper control arm and upper ball joint assembly and disconnect the upper control arm from the steering knuckle.

NOTE: *Do not allow the steering knuckle to hang by the flexible brake line. Wire the steering knuckle up to the frame temporarily.*

4. Remove the two bolts from the upper pivot shaft and remove the upper control arm from the bracket. Be sure to note the position and number of shims used for adjusting the camber and caster angles when removing the upper control arm. This is to ensure that the shims are reinstalled in their original positions.

5. To remove the pivot shaft and bushings from the upper control arm assembly, remove the bushing nuts from the pivot shaft by loosening them alternately, then remove the pivot shaft.

The upper control arm and ball joint assembly

6. To install the upper control arm and ball joint assembly, first install the pivot shaft boots to the pivot shaft.

7. Fill the internal part of the bushings with grease (molybdenum disulfide) and screw the bushings into the pivot shaft. Be sure to screw the right-side and the left-side bushings alternately into the pivot shafts carefully avoiding getting grease on the outer face of the bushings. Tighten the nuts to 250 ft lbs.

NOTE: *Be sure that the control arm and bushings are centered properly and that the control arm rotates with resistance but not binding on the pivot shaft when tightened to the proper torque.*

8. Install the grease fittings and lubricate the parts with grease through the grease fittings.

9. Install the ball joint stud through the steering knuckle. Install the castellated nut and tighten it to 75 ft lbs and just enough additional torque to install the cotter pin. Use a new cotter pin.

10. Mount the upper control arm to the chassis frame and install the shims in their original positions between the pivot shaft and bracket. Tighten the pivot shaft attaching nuts to 55 ft lbs.

NOTE: *Tighten the thinner shim pack's nut first for improved shaft-to-frame clamping force and torque retention.*

11. Install the dust cover.

12. Install the wheel and tire assembly and lower the vehicle to the floor.

LOWER BALL JOINT

Removal and Installation

1. Raise the front of the vehicle and support it with jackstands.

2. Remove the wheel and tire assembly.

3. Remove the cotter pin and castellated nut which retains the ball joint to the steering knuckle.

4. Remove the two bolts retaining the lower ball joint and strut rod.

5. Remove the remaining two bolts.

6. Remove the ball joint.

7. Install the lower ball joint by mounting the joint to the lower control arm and tightening the four bolts to 45 ft lbs.

8. Install the ball joint stud into the steering knuckle and install the cas-

The lower ball joint assembly

tellated nut and torque it to 75 ft lbs and just enough additional torque to align the cotter pin hole with one of the castellations on the nut. Install a new cotter pin.

9. Lubricate the lower ball joint through the grease fitting.

10. Install the wheel and tire assembly and lower the vehicle to the ground.

LOWER CONTROL ARM

Removal and Installation

1. Jack up the vehicle and support it with jackstands.

2. Remove the wheel and tire.

3. Remove the strut bar by removing the frame side bracket and the double nuts, washer and the rubber bushing from the front side of the strut bar. Next, remove the two bolts fastening the strut bar to the lower control arm and remove the bar.

4. Disconnect the stabilizer bar from the lower control arm.

5. Remove the torsion bar.

6. Disconnect the shock absorber from the lower control arm.

7. If you so desire, remove the lower ball joint from the lower control arm joint at this time.

8. Remove the retaining nut and drive out the bolt holding the lower control arm to the chassis with a soft metal drift. Remove the lower control arm from the vehicle.

9. To install the lower control arm, first, install the lower ball joint to the lower control arm. Tighten the retaining nuts to 45 ft lbs.

10. Mount the lower control arm to the frame. Drive the bolt into position carefully with a soft metal drift. Use care not to damage the serrated portions. Tighten the nut on the end of the pivot bolt to 135 ft lbs.

11. Install the stabilizer bar to the lower control arm.

12. Place the washers and bushings on the strut rod and install it through the frame bracket. Install the second set of washers and bushings on the strut rod together with the lockwashers and nut. Leave the nut loose temporarily.

13. Install the strut rod to the lower control arm and tighten the bolts to 45 ft lbs.

The lower control arm assembly

14. Assemble the lower ball joint to the steering knuckle.

15. Install the wheel and tire and lower the vehicle.

16. Tighten the first strut bar-to-chassis frame attaching nut to 175 ft lbs, and the second locknut to 55 ft lbs.

FRONT END ALIGNMENT

Proper alignment of the front wheels must be maintained in order to ensure ease of steering and satisfactory tire life.

The most important factors of front wheel alignment are wheel camber, axle caster, and wheel toe-in.

Wheel toe-in is the distance by which the wheels are closer together at the front than at the rear.

Wheel camber is the amount in which the top of the wheels incline outward from the vertical.

Front axle caster is the amount in degrees which the steering knuckle pivot

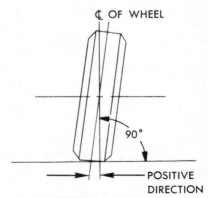

CAMBER ANGLE
LEFT FRONT VIEW

Camber angle as viewed from the left front of the vehicle

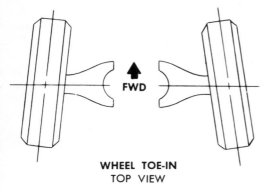

WHEEL TOE-IN
TOP VIEW

Front wheel toe-in as viewed from the top

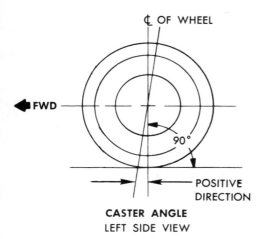

CASTER ANGLE
LEFT SIDE VIEW

Caster angle as viewed from the left-side of the vehicle

axis is tilted toward the rear of the vehicle. Positive caster is the inclination of the top of the steering knuckle toward the rear of the vehicle.

These points should be checked at regular intervals, particularly when the front suspension has been subjected to severe impact. When checking the wheel alignment, it is important that the wheel bearings be properly adjusted and the ball joints have no free-play.

Caster Adjustment

The purpose of caster is to provide steering stability which will keep the front wheels in the straight-ahead position and also assist in straightening up the wheels when coming out of a turn.

The caster is adjusted by adding or subtracting spacer shims from either the front or rear upper control arm pivot shaft attaching bolts.

Camber Adjustment

The purpose of camber is to more nearly place the weight of the vehicle over the tire contact patch on the road to facilitate ease of steering. The result of excessive camber is irregular wear of the tires on the outside shoulder and is usually caused by bent parts. Excessive negative camber will also cause hard steering and possibly wandering. The tires will wear on the inside shoulders.

The camber angle is adjusted by adding or subtracting spacer shims from both the front and rear upper control arm pivot shaft attaching bolts. The same amount of shims is added or subtracted to both of the bolts at the same time.

Toe-In

The toe-in measurement is the difference between the distances between the front and rear center of the tread of the two front tires.

The toe-in can be adjusted by turning the intermediate rod after loosening the locknuts on the intermediate rod ends. The locknuts have left-hand and right-hand threads to allow for equal adjustment of both wheels at the same time. Turn the intermediate rod toward the front of the vehicle to reduce the toe-in angle and toward the rear of the vehicle to increase the toe-in angle.

Wheel Alignment Specifications

| | | CASTER | | CAMBER | | | Steering |
| | | Range (deg) | Preferred Setting (deg) | Range (deg) | Preferred Setting (deg) | Toe-in (in.) | Axis Inclination (deg) |
Year	Model						
All	All	0 to 1P	½P①	½P to 1½P	1P②	+⅛ ±1⁄16③	7

① Caster should not vary more than ½° from side-to-side
② Camber should not vary more than ½° from side-to-side
③ Always adjust the toe-in after adjusting caster and camber

Ride Height Adjustment

NOTE: *The ride height should be measured with a full tank of gas, spare tire, jack, no passengers, and with the tires inflated to the correct pressure.*

1. Place the vehicle on a smooth level floor and bounce the front end several times. Raise the vehicle and then allow it to settle to a normal height.

2. Measure the distance between the bottom of the lower ball joint stud which fits through the steering knuckle and the ground and the distance between the frame crossmember that the lower control arm attaches to and the ground.

The difference between these two measurements should be 2.52 in. (1.54 in. with the vehicle loaded to GVW).

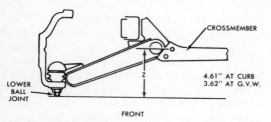

Ride height measurement at the front of the vehicle

3. Adjust the vehicle height by first loosening the nuts on the front end of the strut bar and then turning the vehicle height adjusting bolt. Turn the bolt clockwise to raise the vehicle. As an additional check, measure the clearance between the rubber bumper and the lower control arm. The clearance should be ⅞ in.

4. Check the ride height at the front of the vehicle as outlined in Step 2 above and the ride height at the rear axle by measuring the clearance between the top of the axle and the bottom of the

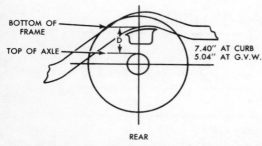

Ride height measurement at the rear of the vehicle

frame where the frame rises to clear the axle. The clearance between the frame and axle at this point should be 7.90 in. (6.26 in. with the vehicle loaded to GVW).

5. After obtaining the correct clearances, securely tighten the strut bar attaching nuts to the proper torque.

Rear Suspension

The rear suspension consists of semi-elliptical leaf springs with hydraulic double-acting shock absorbers. There is a straight "helper" spring added to the bottom of the spring pack. When the semi-elliptical spring straightens out due to the vehicle being loaded, they come in contact with the helper spring which helps to support any additional weight.

SPRINGS

Removal

1. Jack up the rear of the vehicle and place jackstands under the frame near the rear end of the rear spring brackets.

2. Remove the rear shock absorbers.

3. Remove the parking brake cable clips.

4. Remove the nuts from the U-bolts holding the springs to the axle housing.

5. Jack the rear axle up to remove the weight of the axle housing from the springs.

6. Remove the front and rear shackle pin nuts.

7. Drive out the rear shackle pin by using a hammer and drift and lower the rear end of the leaf spring assembly to the floor.

8. Drive out the front shackle pin and remove the leaf spring assembly rearward.

9. Remove the shackle pin from the rear spring bracket and remove the shackle.

Inspection

1. Check the leaf springs for cracks, wear and broken leaves. Replace any leaves found to be cracked, broken, fatigued or seriously worn.

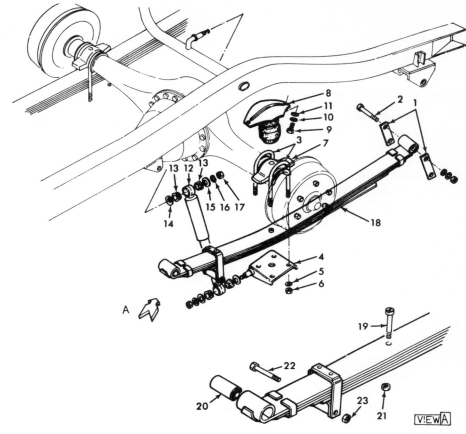

Exploded view of the rear suspension

1. Shackle	7. Seat	13. Bushing	19. Bolt
2. Pin	8. Rubber	14. Washer	20. Bush
3. U-bolt	9. Bolt	15. Washer	21. Nut
4. Clamp	10. Washer	16. Washer	22. Bolt
5. Washer	11. Washer	17. Nut	23. Nut
6. Nut	12. Absorber	18. Spring assy.	

2. Check the shackles for bending and the pins for wear.

3. Check the U-bolts for distortion or other damage.

Installation

1. Mount the shackle to the bracket.

2. Align the front end of the leaf spring assembly with the front bracket and install the shackle pin.

3. Align the rear end of the leaf spring assembly with the shackle and install the shackle pin.

4. Loosely install the shackle pin nuts and install the U-bolts. Tighten the U-bolt nuts to 40 ft lbs.

5. Install the shock absorbers.

6. Clip the parking brake cable to the bracket.

7. Remove the jackstands and lower the vehicle so that the vehicle weight is on the leaf springs.

8. Tighten the shackle pin nuts to 130 ft lbs.

SHOCK ABSORBERS

Removal and Installation

Remove the rear shock absorbers by loosening and removing the upper and lower attaching nuts and pulling the shock absorber ends off the mounting studs, together with the washers and rubber bushings. Install the shock absorbers in the reverse order of removal, making sure that you use new rubber bushings and that they are installed correctly in the bevel shaped mounting holes in the end of the shock absorbers.

Steering

STEERING WHEEL

Removal and Installation

1. Disconnect the battery ground cable.
2. Remove the horn shroud and spring by pushing and turning it counterclockwise. Remove the horn contact ring and wire.
3. Remove the steering wheel-to-steering shaft retaining nut, washer and lockwasher.
4. Mark the relative position of the steering wheel and shaft to each other.
5. Remove the steering column cowling by removing the four attaching screws and washers.
6. Remove the steering wheel from the shaft with a puller.

NOTE: *Under no circumstances is the steering shaft to be hammered upon, jarred, or leaned upon. The steering column is a collapsible, energy-absorbing type and can be easily damaged through mistreatment.*

7. Install the steering wheel in the reverse order of removal, aligning the marks made on the steering wheel and the shaft. Draw the steering wheel onto the shaft with the attaching nut.

TURN SIGNAL AND DIMMER SWITCH

Removal and Installation

1. Disconnect the battery ground cable.
2. Remove the four screws retaining the steering column cowling and remove the cowling.
3. Remove the wire connectors from the switch.
4. Remove the switch by removing the two screws which retain the switch clamp to the steering column mast jacket.
5. Replace the switch in the reverse order of removal.

9 · Brakes

The Chevy LUV is equipped with vacuum assisted hydraulic self-adjusting drum type brakes.

The front brakes are of the two leading shoe type which incorporate two wheel cylinders at each wheel. The front wheel cylinder actuates the lower brake shoe and the rear cylinder the upper brake shoe. The brake linings are molded and bonded to the brake shoes.

The rear brakes are the duo-servo type with a single wheel cylinder on each wheel. The wheel cylinder has two pistons, actuating both the secondary and primary brake shoes. The brake lining is also molded and bonded to the brake shoes. The primary lining is smaller than the secondary lining.

The self-adjusters on the front brakes operate during forward stops and the self-adjusters on the rear brakes adjust on reverse stops.

The parking brake is actuated by a ratchet type L-handle mounted to the dash at the right of the steering column. A cable connects the handle to the intermediate cable by means of a lever. The intermediate cable attaches to the two rear cables which operate the rear service brakes. Adjustment of the parking brake is provided at the equalizer.

Brake System

Adjustment

Although the brakes are self-adjusting, an initial adjusting may be necessary after the brakes have been replaced, or whenever the adjuster position has been changed. The final adjustment is made by using the self-adjusting mechanism.

1. With the brake drum removed, disengage the pullback springs from the adjuster plates on the front brakes, or the actuator from the starwheel on the rear brakes.

2. Using the brake drum as an adjustment gauge, adjust the upper and lower shoes an equal number of notches on the front brakes, or turn the starwheel on the rear brakes until the brake drum slides over the brake shoes with a slight drag.

3. Retract the upper and lower shoes of the front brakes two notches, or turn the starwheel on the rear brakes 1–¼ turns to retract the shoes.

4. Install the brake drums and wheels and lower the vehicle.

NOTE: *If the backing plate access plugs were removed on the front brakes, make sure that they are rein-*

*stalled before making the final adjust-
ment. Also, the brake drums are to be
installed in the same position from
which they were removed. Make sure
that you install the drum-to-flange locating screw.*

5. Perform the final adjustment by
making a number of forward and reverse
stops, applying the brakes with a firm
pedal effort until a satisfactory brake
pedal height, and straight-line braking is
achieved.

Brake Pedal Height Adjustment

When the brake pedal is fully released, the pedal bumper bottoms on the
stop light switch housing.

1. Disconnect the battery ground
cable.

2. Measure the brake pedal height
after making sure that the pedal is fully
returned by the pedal return spring. The
brake pedal height should be between
5.9 and 6.3 in.

3. If it is necessary to adjust the brake
pedal height, disconnect the stop light
switch wiring, remove the switch locknut, and remove the switch from the

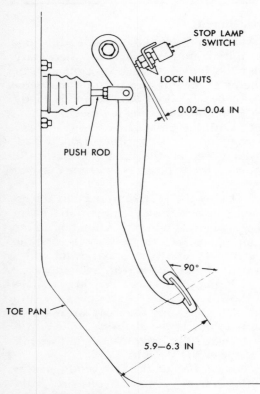

Brake pedal height adjustment

switch bracket by rotating it counterclockwise.

4. Loosen the locknut on the master
cylinder pushrod.

5. Adjust the brake pedal to the specified height by rotating the pushrod in
the appropriate direction. Tighten the
locknut when the proper height is
reached.

6. Install the stop light switch. Adjust
the clearance between the switch housing and the brake pedal tab to 0.03 in.
Tighten the switch locknut.

7. Connect the stop light switch
wires.

8. Connect the battery ground cable.

Hydraulic System

MASTER CYLINDER

Removal and Installation

1. Disconnect the battery ground
cable.

2. Wipe the master cylinder and brake
lines clean. Place absorbent cloths
below the master cylinder area to absorb
any fluid leakage.

3. Disconnect the hydraulic lines at
the connections on the master cylinder.
Cover the ends of the brake lines to prevent the entrance of dirt.

4. Remove the master cylinder bracket
bolt at the front end of the master cylinder.

5. Remove the master cylinder-to-
booster attaching nuts and lockwashers
and remove the master cylinder and
gasket from the booster.

6. Install the master cylinder in the reverse order of removal, and bleed the
brake hydraulic system.

Overhaul

1. Remove the master cylinder from
the vehicle.

2. Remove the fluid reservoir caps,
plates and strainers and drain the fluid
from the reservoirs.

3. Place the master cylinder in a
vise.

4. Loosen the fluid reservoir clamp
screws and remove the plastic reservoirs
from the master cylinder body.

5. Remove the connector bolt, connector and gaskets from the front system side (rear outlet). Then, remove the end plug, gasket, check valve, return spring and spring seat.

6. Remove the connector, gasket, check valve, return spring and spring seat from the rear system side (front outlet).

7. Push the primary piston all the way in and then remove the stopper bolt and gasket on the right-side of the master cylinder.

8. Using snap-ring pliers, remove the primary piston snap-ring.

9. Remove the primary and secondary piston assemblies from the cylinder bore.

10. Clean all of the parts in clean brake fluid. Blow out all passages, orifices, and valve holes with compressed air.

11. Inspect the master cylinder bore and pistons for scoring, corrosion, and rust. Slight scoring and rust can be re-

moved by polishing with crocus cloth or fine emery paper soaked with brake fluid.

12. Soak all new and old parts in clean brake fluid before reassembling.

13. Insert the secondary piston assembly into the master cylinder bore, so that the primary stem guide is projected slightly beyond the cylinder bore end.

14. Insert the primary piston into the master cylinder bore so that the secondary piston stem guide enters the hole in the primary piston.

15. Install the snap-ring into the groove in the master cylinder housing.

16. Depress the primary piston and install the piston stopper bolt and new gasket.

17. Install the spring seat, return spring, check valve, new gasket and end plug in the front system side of the master cylinder (rear outlet).

18. Install a new gasket on either side of the connector and secure it into position with the connector bolt.

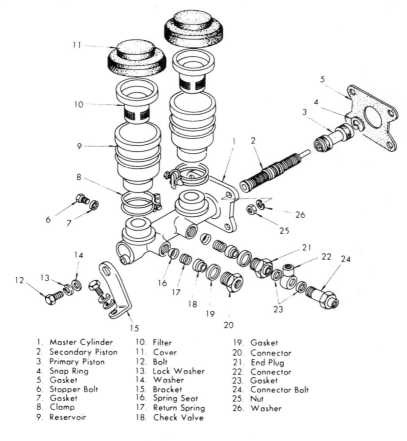

1. Master Cylinder	10. Filter	19. Gasket
2. Secondary Piston	11. Cover	20. Connector
3. Primary Piston	12. Bolt	21. End Plug
4. Snap Ring	13. Lock Washer	22. Connector
5. Gasket	14. Washer	23. Gasket
6. Stopper Bolt	15. Bracket	24. Connector Bolt
7. Gasket	16. Spring Seat	25. Nut
8. Clamp	17. Return Spring	26. Washer
9. Reservoir	18. Check Valve	

Exploded view of the master cylinder

19. Install the spring seat, return spring, check valve, new gasket and connector in the rear system side of the master cylinder (front outlet).

20. Install the clamps over the lower ends of the fluid reservoirs, place the reservoirs in position on the master cylinder body and then tighten the clamp bolts.

21. Install the reservoir filters, and fill the reservoirs with clean brake fluid. Push in on the primary piston to determine that it returns smoothly. Test the piston assembly two or three times to make sure that fluid comes out of the front and rear outlets.

22. Install the plates and covers.

23. Install plugs in all of the connector outlet ports.

24. Fill the reservoirs to the proper level with clean brake fluid.

25. Insert a rod with a smooth round end to the piston end and press it in to compress the piston return spring.

26. Release the pressure on the rod. Watch for air bubbles in the reservoir fluid.

27. Repeat Steps 25 and 26 as long as bubbles appear in the fluid.

28. Install the master cylinder on the vehicle and bleed the brake hydraulic system.

Bleeding

The brake hydraulic system must be bled after any line has been disconnected or air has somehow found its way into the system.

The bleeding operation should start with the wheel cylinder nearest the master cylinder and end with the one farthest away

NOTE: *Do not bleed the brakes with the brake drums removed.*

1. Make sure that the master cylinder is full and kept at least ¾ full throughout the entire bleeding process. Check the fluid level in the master cylinder reservoirs frequently during the bleeding operation.

2. Remove the cap from the wheel cylinder bleeder valve. Position a wrench on the bleeder valve and place a rubber hose over the bleeder valve nipple.

3. Place the other end of the bleeder hose into a clear container containing

Bleeding the brake hydraulic system

enough brake fluid to ensure that the end of the bleeder hose will remain submerged.

4. Start the engine and allow it to run during the actual bleeding of each wheel cylinder. This is so to have vacuum applied to the brake booster during the bleeding process.

5. Open the wheel cylinder bleeder valve by turning the wrench counterclockwise about ¾ of a turn. Have an assistant depress the brake pedal. Just before the brake pedal reaches the end of its travel, close the bleeder valve and allow the brake pedal to return slowly to the released position. Repeat this operation until the brake fluid being expelled is free from air bubbles, then close the bleeder valve tightly.

6. Remove the bleeder hose and the wrench from the bleeder valve and install them onto the next wheel cylinder to be bled. Repeat Step 5 on all of the remaining wheel cylinders. Don't forget to check and replenish the brake fluid in the master cylinder reservoirs.

7. After bleeding the brake hydraulic system, check the operation of the brakes. Depress the brake pedal several times then hold it depressed. Notice how far the pedal can be depressed. Release the pedal for about 10 seconds, then depress it again and hold it, taking notice of the distance which it can be depressed before it stops with the same amount of pedal pressure applied as before. If the pedal depresses further or can be "pumped up," then it can be as-

sumed that there is still air in the hydraulic system and further bleeding is required.

Front Drum Brakes

BRAKE DRUMS

Removal and Installation

1. Jack up the vehicle and support it on jackstands.

2. Remove the wheel cover and remove the wheel and tire assembly.

3. Remove the brake drum and hub retaining screws and remove the drum. Identify the drum so that it can be reinstalled in the same position.

If the brake drums are worn considerably, it may be necessary to retract the brake shoes before the drum can be removed. Remove the rubber hole plugs in the backing plate and insert a screwdriver through the hole and into the hole in the brake shoe. Raise the end of the brake shoe return spring to release it from the serration and contact the brake shoe by moving it in toward the wheel cylinder.

NOTE: *Never depress the brake pedal while the brake drums are removed.*

4. Install the brake drums in the reverse order of removal.

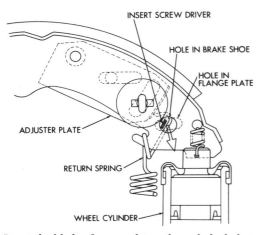

Insert the blade of a screwdriver through the hole in the backing plate and the brake shoe, raise and release the end of the return spring and move the brake shoe in toward the wheel cylinder

Inspection

After removing the brake drum, remove any dirt and inspect the drum for cracks, deep grooves, roughness, scoring, or out-of-roundness. Replace any brake drum which is cracked completely through.

Smooth any slight scores by polishing the friction surface with fine emery cloth. Heavy or extensive scoring will cause excessive brake lining wear and should be removed from the brake drum through resurfacing of the brake drum friction surface. The maximum finished diameter of the brake drums must not exceed 10.059 in. The brake drum must be replaced if the diameter is 10.079 in. or greater.

BRAKE SHOES

Removal and Installation

The brake linings must be replaced when the lining thickness is 0.059 in. or less.

1. Remove the brake drum.

2. Disconnect the wheel cylinder piston springs from the pistons and shoes with a pair of pliers.

3. Depress and rotate the hold-down spring retainers 90° with a pair of pliers and then remove the springs and retainers.

4. Remove the upper and lower brake shoes.

5. Depress the self-adjusting spring retainers, rotate the shoe 90° while holding the retainer and then separate the self-adjuster retainer, washer, spring,

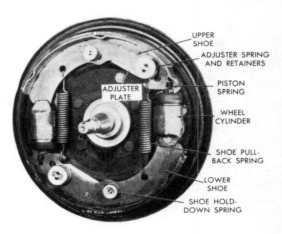

Front brake assembly components

Removing the wheel cylinder piston springs

Removing the hold-down spring retainers and springs

pin, adjuster lever and the brake shoe from each other.

NOTE: *If the shoes, adjuster levers and return springs are to be reinstalled, be sure to mark their location so that they will be reinstalled in their original positions.*

6. Before you install the brake shoes, make sure that your hands and tools are free from grease and oil that could possibly contaminate the brake linings.

7. Place the brake shoe in an arbor press or similar tool and install the adjuster pivot pin, adjuster lever, washer, spring and retainers to each brake shoe. Compress the spring and rotate the retainer 90° while compressing the spring, making sure that the pin end is seated in the retainer groove.

NOTE: *Install the washer so that its lining side is facing the lever. Also, the left and right-side adjuster levers*

are not interchangeable and must be reinstalled in their original positions.

8. Lubricate the brake shoe contact points on the backing plate and the wheel cylinder contact points on the brake shoes with Lubriplate®.

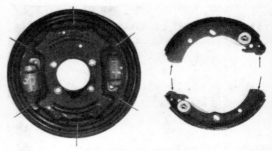

→ LUBRICATION POINTS

Lubrication points for the front brakes

9. Hook the return springs to the brake shoes. Be sure to install the left and right springs in their original positions as they are not interchangeable. The left springs are light blue; right springs are black.

10. Fit the grooved portion of the adjuster lever to the guide pin and install the brake shoes in position. Make sure that the shoes are fitted properly to the guide pin. If the end of the brake shoe is not inserted in the groove, it is an indication that the brake shoes are lifted off the ridged portion. Make sure that the return spring end is fitted properly to the adjuster lever.

11. Install the piston springs on the wheel cylinder piston ends.

12. Install the brake shoe hold-down springs and retainers. With a pair of pliers, compress the spring and rotate the retainer 90°, making sure that the pin end is seated in the retainer groove.

13. Reinstall the brake drum and adjust the brakes.

WHEEL CYLINDERS

Removal and Installation

It is not necessary to remove the wheel cylinders from the backing plates to disassemble, inspect, and overhaul the cylinder. Removal is necessary only when the wheel cylinder is damaged beyond repair and must be replaced.

It is a good practice to inspect the wheel cylinders for leakage whenever the brake drums are removed. Simply pull the edge of the wheel cylinder boot carefully away from the cylinder and note whether or not the interior is wet with brake fluid. Excessive fluid at this point indicates leakage past the piston cup, requiring overhaul or replacement. A slight amount of fluid present on the inside of the wheel cylinder is almost always present and acts as a lubricant for the piston.

1. Remove the wheel and tire assembly, the brake drum and the brake shoes.

2. Disconnect the brake system hydraulic line from the wheel cylinder at the rear of the backing plate.

3. Remove the screws securing the wheel cylinder to the backing plate and remove the wheel cylinder from the backing plate.

4. Install the wheel cylinder in the reverse order of removal and bleed the brake hydraulic system.

Overhaul

1. Either with the wheel cylinder removed or still on the brake backing plate, remove the boot(s) from the cylinder end(s).

2. Remove the piston(s) and cup(s).

NOTE: *The front wheel cylinder pistons and cups are serviced as an assembly.*

3. Inspect the cylinder bore. Check for staining and corrosion. Discard any wheel cylinder which is excessively corroded. Inspect the piston and discard it if it is excessively pitted, scored or damaged.

4. Polish any stained or slightly scored areas in the cylinder bore with crocus cloth. Move the crocus cloth in a circular motion around the circumference of the cylinder bore, not in a lengthwise manner.

5. Wash the master cylinder body thoroughly in clean brake fluid, allowing it to remain lubricated for assembly. Do not lubricate the pistons or cups prior to their installation in the cylinder.

6. On front wheel cylinders, install the piston assembly into the cylinder, being careful not to damage the boot.

7. On rear wheel cylinders, insert the spring-expander into the cylinder bore. Install the new cups with the flat surface

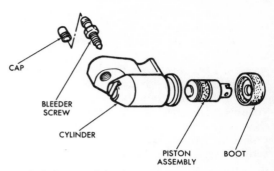

Exploded view of the front wheel cylinder

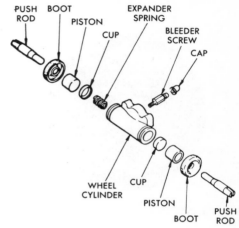

Exploded view of the rear wheel cylinder

toward the outer ends of the cylinder. Be sure that the cups are lint-free. Do not lubricate the cups prior to installation. Install the new pistons into the cylinder with the flat surfaces toward the center of the cylinder. Do not lubricate prior to installation.

8. Press the new boot(s) onto the wheel cylinder.

9. Install the wheel cylinder onto the brake backing plate, if it was removed, assemble the brake shoes to the backing plate, install the brake drum and bleed the brake hydraulic system.

Rear Drum Brakes

BRAKE DRUMS

Removal and Installation

1. Raise the vehicle and support it on jackstands.

2. Remove the hub caps and remove the rear tire and wheel.

3. Loosen the check nuts at the parking brake equalizer sufficiently to remove all tension from the brake cable.

4. Remove the drum-to-hub retaining screws and remove the drum from the vehicle. Identify each brake drum so that it can be reinstalled in its original position. Never depress the brake pedal while any of the brake drums are removed.

5. Install the brake drums in the reverse order of removal.

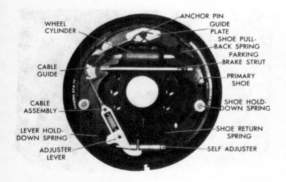

Rear brake assembly components

Inspection

Inspect the rear brake drums in the same manner as is outlined for the front brake drums.

BRAKE SHOES

Removal and Installation

1. Remove the brake drums.
2. Unhook the brake return springs

Removing the brake shoe return springs with a brake tool

from the anchor pin using a brake tool and remove the springs.

3. Remove the brake shoe hold-down springs using pliers. Depress the spring retainer while rotating it 90° to align the slot in the retainer with the flanged end of the pin.

4. Remove the self-adjuster cable assembly by disconnecting the spring at the adjuster lever and removing the cable end from the anchor pin. Remove the guide plate from the anchor pin.

5. Remove the adjuster lever and the lever hold-down wire from the shoe pivot.

6. Separate the shoes from the wheel cylinder pushrods.

7. Separate the primary and secondary brake shoes, adjuster, return spring, and parking brake strut assemblies.

NOTE: *If the brake shoes are to be reinstalled, be sure to identify them so that they can be reinstalled in their original positions.*

8. Separate the parking brake lever and the rear cable. Remove the clip and washer and remove the parking brake lever from the secondary shoe.

9. Lubricate the parking brake cable with Lubriplate®.

10. Assemble the parking brake lever to the secondary shoe and then assemble the parking brake cable to the lever.

11. Before installation, make sure that the adjusting screw is clean, lubricated and operable.

12. Connect the brake shoes together with bottom return spring and then place the adjuster screw into position. The adjuster screw is installed with the starwheel nearest to the secondary shoe.

13. Assemble the parking brake strut with the spring on the primary shoe end, and assemble the shoes to the wheel cylinder pushrods.

14. Install the shoe hold-down springs using a pair of pliers. Compress the springs and rotate the retainers 90°.

15. Install the guide plate on the anchor pin. Assemble the self-adjuster lever and the lever hold-down wire to the secondary shoe pivot pin. Place the adjuster cable over the anchor pin, route the cable around the shoe shield and then attach the spring at the opposite end to the adjuster lever.

Installing the brake shoe return springs with a brake tool

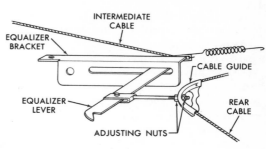

Parking brake adjusting mechanism

16. Install the return springs using a brake tool.

17. Pry the shoes away from the backing plate and lubricate the shoe contact areas with a thin coat of Lubriplate.

18. Check the operation of the parking brake. *Do not step on the brake pedal.*

19. Install the brake drum and adjust the brake shoes.

WHEEL CYLINDERS

Removal and Installation

Remove and install the rear wheel cylinders in the same manner as outlined for the front wheel cylinders.

Overhaul

Follow the procedure given for overhauling the front wheel cylinders to overhaul the rear wheel cylinders.

Parking Brake

Adjustment

Since the rear brakes are utilized as service brakes and parking brakes, the service brake must be properly adjusted as a base for parking brake adjustment and conversely, the parking brake must be properly adjusted for the service brakes to operate properly.

1. Raise the vehicle on a hoist.

2. Apply the parking brake two notches from the fully released position.

3. Loosen the equalizer check nut, and tighten or loosen the front jam nut until a light to moderate drag is felt when the rear wheels are rotated frontward.

4. Tighten the nuts securely. Hold the front nut while tightening the jam nut.

5. Fully release the parking brake and rotate the rear wheels. No drag should be present.

6. Lower the vehicle.

PARKING BRAKE CABLES

Removal and Installation

FRONT CABLE

1. Disconnect the battery ground cable.

2. Remove the carburetor air cleaner.

3. Drain the cooling system. Disconnect the heater hoses at the heater core outlet tubes at the dash panel and secure the hoses in an upright position to minimize coolant loss.

4. Disconnect the parking brake front cable at the control lever on the right-side of the engine compartment.

5. Remove the right-hand pulley center bolt and remove the pulley.

6. Remove the cable cover nuts at the dash panel and remove the cover.

7. Remove the windshield wiper switch on the instrument panel.

8. Remove the screws attaching the lever assembly to the instrument panel.

9. Pull the assembly rearward and lay it on the floor.

10. Loosen the parking brake light switch bracket screw and rotate the switch and bracket 90°.

11. Manually release the ratchet and then depress the handle all the way in.

12. Remove the cotter pin, washer, pivot pin and the pulley. Remove the cable assembly.

13. Install the cable to handle lower end and then pull the handle rearward several notches.

14. Rotate the parking brake light switch and bracket into position and tighten the bracket screw.

15. Install the pulley, pivot pin, washer and cotter pin.

16. For the remainder of the installation procedure follow the removal procedure in reverse starting with Step 8.

INTERMEDIATE CABLE

1. Raise the vehicle on a hoist.

2. Disconnect the equalizer lever spring at the lever.

3. Loosen the cable guide nut and remove the cable assembly.

4. Install the intermediate cable in the reverse order of removal and adjust the parking brake.

REAR CABLE

1. Raise the vehicle on a hoist.

2. Remove the rear cable retaining clamps on the left and right-sides.

3. Disconnect the equalizer lever return spring at the lever.

4. Remove the cotter pin, washer and pin and remove the equalizer lever from the front cable and equalizer adjusting bolt clevis.

5. Remove the left and right rear wheel and tire assemblies.

6. Remove the brake drums and shoes, disconnecting the rear cable from the brake lever.

7. Remove the rear cable spring cup using a box wrench.

8. Withdraw the cable ends from the backing plates on either side and remove the cable assembly.

9. Install the cable in the reverse order of removal and adjust the parking brake.

Removing the rear cable spring cup at the backing plate

Brake Specifications

(All measurements are given in in.)

Year	Model	Master Cylinder Bore	Wheel Cylinder Bore		Brake Drum Diameter		Minimum Lining Thickness
			Front	Rear	Front	Rear	
1972–75	All	0.875	1.06	0.75	10.0	10.0	0.059

10 · Body

Doors

Removal and Installation

1. Support the door with a jackstand or jack with a block of wood between the lower part of the door panel and the supporting device.
2. Take out the bolts retaining the door hinges and remove the door.
3. Install the door in the reverse order of removal.

DOOR PANEL

Removal and Installation

1. Depress the door panel assembly at the window regulator handle enough to take out the window regulator handle clip and remove the regulator handle.
2. Remove the inside lever escutcheon by raising the lever and pulling the escutcheon.
3. Remove the door arm rest pad assembly.
4. Remove the nine nylon bullet-type fasteners that retain the door panel and remove the door panel.
5. Install the door panel in the reverse order of removal. Be sure to insert the snap-ring into the slot in the handle before installing the window regulator handle.

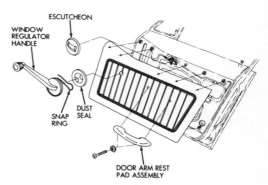

The door panel assembly

WINDOWS

Removal and Installation

1. Remove the door panel and peel off the water deflectors.
2. Remove the glass stopper and then remove the window glass from the door regulator.
3. Remove the inside lever assembly.
4. Remove the glass run channel.
5. Take out the glass by lowering it to the bottom and lifting its side up.
6. To install the window glass, reverse the above procedure.

DOOR LOCKS

Removal and Installation

1. Remove the door panel and peel off the water deflectors on the check holes.

Removing the door window glass

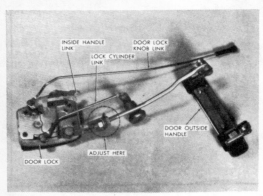

The door lock assembly

2. Take out the clip from the door lock side of the inside lever assembly.

3. Remove the cylinder link from the lock cylinder.

4. Remove the glass run channel.

5. Remove the relay lever bracket at the door lock side.

6. Remove the door lock button.

7. Separate the outer link from the outside handle link and then remove the screws attaching the door lock assembly.

8. Remove the door lock from the door.

9. To replace the door lock, install the door lock in position.

10. Install the door lock knob.

11. Connect the door outside handle with the door lock link and loosely install the bolts.

12. Adjust the linkage so that there is ¼ in. or less of free-play in the handle,

then secure the link with an open-end wrench.

13. Connect the door lock link to the lock cylinder.

14. Mount the glass run channel and support bracket.

15. Install the inside lever assembly in position and connect it to the door lock link.

16. Install the door panel.

LOCK CYLINDER ASSEMBLY

Removal and Installation

1. Remove the door panel and partially detach the inner panel water deflector. Raise the door window. Detach the door lock link.

2. With a screwdriver, slide the lock cylinder retaining clip on the door outer panel out of engagement and remove the lock cylinder from the door.

3. Install the lock cylinder in the reverse order of removal.

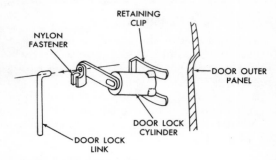

The door lock cylinder assembly

Hood

Alignment

The position of the hood in relation to the body and fenders (vertical height) can be adjusted by moving the position of the hinges where they are secured to the body of the vehicle.

The fore and aft position of the hood can be adjusted by moving the position of the hinges where they are attached to the hood.

Adjust the position of the hood latch by loosening the retaining screws and making the necessary vertical and horizontal adjustments. Tighten the screws when finished.

Fuel Tank

Removal and Installation

1. Disconnect the battery ground cable.

2. Remove the fuel filler cap and take out the fuel filter pipe bracket bolts.

3. Disconnect the sending unit from the fuel tank terminal.

4. Unfasten the clips and disconnect the two rubber hoses from the check relief valve to the fuel filter on the front side of the fuel tank.

5. Remove the three fuel tank mounting bolts on the front side and the three mounting bolts on the rear side.

6. Remove the fuel tank from the vehicle.

7. Install the fuel tank in the reverse order of removal.

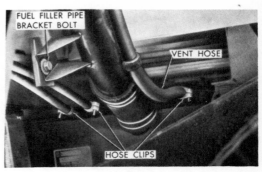

Location of the fuel filler pipe bracket, check relief valve and the vent hoses

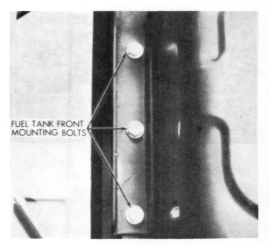

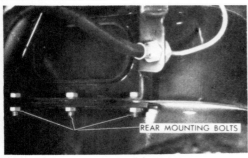

The rear fuel tank mounting bolts

The front fuel tank mounting bolts

Appendix

General Conversion Table

Multiply by	To convert	To	
2.54	Inches	Centimeters	.3937
30.48	Feet	Centimeters	.0328
.914	Yards	Meters	1.094
1.609	Miles	Kilometers	.621
.645	Square inches	Square cm.	.155
.836	Square yards	Square meters	1.196
16.39	Cubic inches	Cubic cm.	.061
28.3	Cubic feet	Liters	.0353
.4536	Pounds	Kilograms	2.2045
4.546	Gallons	Liters	.22
.068	Lbs./sq. in. (psi)	Atmospheres	14.7
.138	Foot pounds	Kg. m.	7.23
1.014	H.P. (DIN)	H.P. (SAE)	.9861
——	To obtain	From	Multiply by

Note: 1 cm. equals 10 mm.; 1 mm. equals .0394″.

Conversion—Common Fractions to Decimals and Millimeters

INCHES			INCHES			INCHES		
Common Fractions	Decimal Fractions	Millimeters (approx.)	Common Fractions	Decimal Fractions	Millimeters (approx.)	Common Fractions	Decimal Fractions	Millimeters (approx.)
1/128	.008	0.20	11/32	.344	8.73	43/64	.672	17.07
1/64	.016	0.40	23/64	.359	9.13	11/16	.688	17.46
1/32	.031	0.79	3/8	.375	9.53	45/64	.703	17.86
3/64	.047	1.19	25/64	.391	9.92	23/32	.719	18.26
1/16	.063	1.59	13/32	.406	10.32	47/64	.734	18.65
5/64	.078	1.98	27/64	.422	10.72	3/4	.750	19.05
3/32	.094	2.38	7/16	.438	11.11	49/64	.766	19.45
7/64	.109	2.78	29/64	.453	11.51	25/32	.781	19.84
1/8	.125	3.18	15/32	.469	11.91	51/64	.797	20.24
9/64	.141	3.57	31/64	.484	12.30	13/16	.813	20.64
5/32	.156	3.97	1/2	.500	12.70	53/64	.828	21.03
11/64	.172	4.37	33/64	.516	13.10	27/32	.844	21.43
3/16	.188	4.76	17/32	.531	13.49	55/64	.859	21.83
13/64	.203	5.16	35/64	.547	13.89	7/8	.875	22.23
7/32	.219	5.56	9/16	.563	14.29	57/64	.891	22.62
15/64	.234	5.95	37/64	.578	14.68	29/32	.906	23.02
1/4	.250	6.35	19/32	.594	15.08	59/64	.922	23.42
17/64	.266	6.75	39/64	.609	15.48	15/16	.938	23.81
9/32	.281	7.14	5/8	.625	15.88	61/64	.953	24.21
19/64	.297	7.54	41/64	.641	16.27	31/32	.969	24.61
5/16	.313	7.94	21/32	.656	16.67	63/64	.984	25.00
21/64	.328	8.33						

Conversion—Millimeters to Decimal Inches

mm	inches	mm	inches	mm	inches	mm	inches	mm	inches
1	.039 370	31	1.220 470	61	2.401 570	91	3.582 670	210	8.267 700
2	.078 740	32	1.259 840	62	2.440 940	92	3.622 040	220	8.661 400
3	.118 110	33	1.299 210	63	2.480 310	93	3.661 410	230	9.055 100
4	.157 480	34	1.338 580	64	2.519 680	94	3.700 780	240	9.448 800
5	.196 850	35	1.377 949	65	2.559 050	95	3.740 150	250	9.842 500
6	.236 220	36	1.417 319	66	2.598 420	96	3.779 520	260	10.236 200
7	.275 590	37	1.456 689	67	2.637 790	97	3.818 890	270	10.629 900
8	.314 960	38	1.496 050	68	2.677 160	98	3.858 260	280	11.032 600
9	.354 330	39	1.535 430	69	2.716 530	99	3.897 630	290	11.417 300
10	.393 700	40	1.574 800	70	2.755 900	100	3.937 000	300	11.811 000
11	.433 070	41	1.614 170	71	2.795 270	105	4.133 848	310	12.204 700
12	.472 440	42	1.653 540	72	2.834 640	110	4.330 700	320	12.598 400
13	.511 810	43	1.692 910	73	2.874 010	115	4.527 550	330	12.992 100
14	.551 180	44	1.732 280	74	2.913 380	120	4.724 400	340	13.385 800
15	.590 550	45	1.771 650	75	2.952 750	125	4.921 250	350	13.779 500
16	.629 920	46	1.811 020	76	2.992 120	130	5.118 100	360	14.173 200
17	.669 290	47	1.850 390	77	3.031 490	135	5.314 950	370	14.566 900
18	.708 660	48	1.889 760	78	3.070 860	140	5.511 800	380	14.960 600
19	.748 030	49	1.929 130	79	3.110 230	145	5.708 650	390	15.354 300
20	.787 400	50	1.968 500	80	3.149 600	150	5.905 500	400	15.748 000
21	.826 770	51	2.007 870	81	3.188 970	155	6.102 350	500	19.685 000
22	.866 140	52	2.047 240	82	3.228 340	160	6.299 200	600	23.622 000
23	.905 510	53	2.086 610	83	3.267 710	165	6.496 050	700	27.559 000
24	.944 880	54	2.125 980	84	3.307 080	170	6.692 900	800	31.496 000
25	.984 250	55	2.165 350	85	3.346 450	175	6.889 750	900	35.433 000
26	1.023 620	56	2.204 720	86	3.385 820	180	7.086 600	1000	39.370 000
27	1.062 990	57	2.244 090	87	3.425 190	185	7.283 450	2000	78.740 000
28	1.102 360	58	2.283 460	88	3.464 560	190	7.480 300	3000	118.110 000
29	1.141 730	59	2.322 830	89	3.503 903	195	7.677 150	4000	157.480 000
30	1.181 100	60	2.362 200	90	3.543 300	200	7.874 000	5000	196.850 000

To change decimal millimeters to decimal inches, position the decimal point where desired on either side of the millimeter measurement shown and reset the inches decimal by the same number of digits in the same direction. For example, to convert .001 mm into decimal inches, reset the decimal behind the 1 mm (shown on the chart) to .001; change the decimal inch equivalent (.039″ shown to .000039″).

Tap Drill Sizes

National Fine or S.A.E.			National Coarse or U.S.S.		
Screw & Tap Size	Threads Per Inch	Use Drill Number	Screw & Tap Size	Threads Per Inch	Use Drill Number
No. 5	44	37	No. 5	40	39
No. 6	40	33	No. 6	32	36
No. 8	36	29	No. 8	32	29
No. 10	32	21	No. 10	24	25
No. 12	28	15	No. 12	24	17
$1/4$	28	3	$1/4$	20	8
$5/16$	24	1	$5/16$	18	F
$3/8$	24	Q	$3/8$	16	$5/16$
$7/16$	20	W	$7/16$	14	U
$1/2$	20	$29/64$	$1/2$	13	$27/64$
$9/16$	18	$33/64$	$9/16$	12	$31/64$
$5/8$	18	$37/64$	$5/8$	11	$17/32$
$3/4$	16	$11/16$	$3/4$	10	$21/32$
$7/8$	14	$13/16$	$7/8$	9	$49/64$
$1 1/8$	12	$1 3/64$	1	8	$7/8$
$1 1/4$	12	$1 11/64$	$1 1/8$	7	$63/64$
$1 1/2$	12	$1 27/64$	$1 1/4$	7	$1 7/64$
			$1 1/2$	6	$1 11/32$

Decimal Equivalent Size of the Number Drills

Drill No.	Decimal Equivalent	Drill No.	Decimal Equivalent	Drill No.	Decimal Equivalent
80	.0135	53	.0595	26	.1470
79	.0145	52	.0635	25	.1495
78	.0160	51	.0670	24	.1520
77	.0180	50	.0700	23	.1540
76	.0200	49	.0730	22	.1570
75	.0210	48	.0760	21	.1590
74	.0225	47	.0785	20	.1610
73	.0240	46	.0810	19	.1660
72	.0250	45	.0820	18	.1695
71	.0260	44	.0860	17	.1730
70	.0280	43	.0890	16	.1770
69	.0292	42	.0935	15	.1800
68	.0310	41	.0960	14	.1820
67	.0320	40	.0980	13	.1850
66	.0330	39	.0995	12	.1890
65	.0350	38	.1015	11	.1910
64	.0360	37	.1040	10	.1935
63	.0370	36	.1065	9	.1960
62	.0380	35	.1100	8	.1990
61	.0390	34	.1110	7	.2010
60	.0400	33	.1130	6	.2040
59	.0410	32	.1160	5	.2055
58	.0420	31	.1200	4	.2090
57	.0430	30	.1285	3	.2130
56	.0465	29	.1360	2	.2210
55	.0520	28	.1405	1	.2280
54	.0550	27	.1440		

Decimal Equivalent Size of the Letter Drills

Letter Drill	Decimal Equivalent	Letter Drill	Decimal Equivalent	Letter Drill	Decimal Equivalent
A	.234	J	.277	S	.348
B	.238	K	.281	T	.358
C	.242	L	.290	U	.368
D	.246	M	.295	V	.377
E	.250	N	.302	W	.386
F	.257	O	.316	X	.397
G	.261	P	.323	Y	.404
H	.266	Q	.332	Z	.413
I	.272	R	.339		

ANTI-FREEZE INFORMATION

Freezing and Boiling Points of Solutions
According to Percentage of Alcohol or Ethylene Glycol

Freezing Point of Solation	Alcohol Volume %	Alcohol Solution Boils at	Ethylene Glycol Volume %	Ethylene Glycol Solution Boils at
20°F.	12	196°F.	16	216°F.
10°F.	20	189°F.	25	218°F.
0°F.	27	184°F.	33	220°F.
−10°F.	32	181°F.	39	222°F.
−20°F.	38	178°F.	44	224°F.
−30°F.	42	176°F.	48	225°F.

Note: above boiling points are at sea level. For every 1,000 feet of altitude, boiling points are approximately 2°F. lower than those shown. For every pound of pressure exerted by the pressure cap, the boiling points are approximately 3°F. higher than those shown.

ANTI-FREEZE CHART

Temperatures Shown in Degrees Fahrenheit
+32 is Freezing

Cooling System Capacity Quarts	Quarts of ETHYLENE GLYCOL Needed for Protection to Temperatures Shown Below													
	1	2	3	4	5	6	7	8	9	10	11	12	13	14
10	+24°	+16°	+ 4°	−12°	−34°	−62°								
11	+25	+18	+ 8	− 6	−23	−47								
12	+26	+19	+10	0	−15	−34	−57°							
13	+27	+21	+13	+ 3	− 9	−25	−45							
14			+15	+ 6	− 5	−18	−34							
15			+16	+ 8	0	−12	−26							
16			+17	+10	+ 2	− 8	−19	−34	−52°					
17			+18	+12	+ 5	− 4	−14	−27	−42					
18			+19	+14	+ 7	0	−10	−21	−34	−50°				
19			+20	+15	+ 9	+ 2	− 7	−16	−28	−42				
20				+16	+10	+ 4	− 3	−12	−22	−34	−48°			
21				+17	+12	+ 6	0	− 9	−17	−28	−41			
22				+18	+13	+ 8	+ 2	− 6	−14	−23	−34	−47°		
23				+19	+14	+ 9	+ 4	− 3	−10	−19	−29	−40		
24				+19	+15	+10	+ 5	0	− 8	−15	−23	−34	−46°	
25				+20	+16	+12	+ 7	+ 1	− 5	−12	−20	−29	−40	−50°
26					+17	+13	+ 8	+ 3	− 3	− 9	−16	−25	−34	−44
27					+18	+14	+ 9	+ 5	− 1	− 7	−13	−21	−29	−39
28					+18	+15	+10	+ 6	+ 1	− 5	−11	−18	−25	−34
29					+19	+16	+12	+ 7	+ 2	− 3	− 8	−15	−22	−29
30					+20	+17	+13	+ 8	+ 4	− 1	− 6	−12	−18	−25

For capacities over 30 quarts divide true capacity by 3. Find quarts Anti-Freeze for the 1/3 and multiply by 3 for quarts to add.

For capacities under 10 quarts multiply true capacity by 3. Find quarts Anti-Freeze for the tripled volume and divide by 3 for quarts to add.

To Increase the Freezing Protection of Anti-Freeze Solutions Already Installed

Cooling System Capacity Quarts	Number of Quarts of ETHYLENE GLYCOL Anti-Freeze Required to Increase Protection													
	From +20°F. to					From +10°F. to					From 0°F. to			
	0°	−10°	−20°	−30°	−40°	0°	−10°	−20°	−30°	−40°	−10°	−20°	−30°	−40°
10	1 3/4	2 1/4	3	3 1/2	3 3/4	3/4	1 1/2	2 1/4	2 3/4	3 1/4	3/4	1 1/2	2	2 1/2
12	2	2 3/4	3 1/2	4	4 1/2	1	1 3/4	2 1/2	3 1/4	3 3/4	1	1 3/4	2 1/2	3 1/4
14	2 1/4	3 1/4	4	4 3/4	5 1/2	1 1/4	2	3	3 3/4	4 1/2	1	2	3	3 1/2
16	2 1/2	3 1/2	4 1/2	5 1/4	6	1 1/4	2 1/2	3 1/2	4 1/4	5 1/4	1 1/4	2 1/4	3 1/4	4
18	3	4	5	6	7	1 1/2	2 3/4	4	5	5 3/4	1 1/2	2 1/2	3 3/4	4 3/4
20	3 1/4	4 1/2	5 3/4	6 3/4	7 1/2	1 3/4	3	4 1/4	5 1/2	6 1/2	1 1/2	2 3/4	4 1/4	5 1/4
22	3 1/2	5	6 1/4	7 1/4	8 1/4	1 3/4	3 1/4	4 3/4	6	7 1/4	1 3/4	3 1/4	4 1/2	5 1/2
24	4	5 1/2	7	8	9	2	3 1/2	5	6 1/2	7 1/2	1 3/4	3 1/2	5	6
26	4 1/4	6	7 1/2	8 3/4	10	2	4	5 1/2	7	8 1/4	2	3 3/4	5 1/2	6 3/4
28	4 1/2	6 1/4	8	9 1/2	10 1/2	2 1/4	4 1/4	6	7 1/2	9	2	4	5 3/4	7 1/4
30	5	6 3/4	8 1/2	10	11 1/2	2 1/2	4 1/2	6 1/2	8	9 1/2	2 1/4	4 1/4	6 1/4	7 3/4

Test radiator solution with proper hydrometer. Determine from the table the number of quarts of solution to be drawn off from a full cooling system and replace with undiluted anti-freeze, to give the desired increased protection. For example, to increase protection of a 22-quart cooling system containing Ethylene Glycol (permanent type) anti-freeze, from +20°F. to −20°F. will require the replacement of 6 1/4 quarts of solution with undiluted anti-freeze.